Changes in the Higher Education Sector

Changes in the Higher Education Sector

Contemporary Drivers and the Pursuit of Excellence

Khalid Khan, Dawne Gurbutt
and Rachel Cragg

ANTHEM PRESS

Anthem Press
An imprint of Wimbledon Publishing Company
www.anthempress.com

This edition first published in UK and USA 2022
by ANTHEM PRESS
75–76 Blackfriars Road, London SE1 8HA, UK
or PO Box 9779, London SW19 7ZG, UK
and
244 Madison Ave #116, New York, NY 10016, USA

British Library Cataloguing-in-Publication Data
A catalogue record for this book is available from the British Library.

Library of Congress Control Number: 2021953405

ISBN-13: 978-1-83998-197-5 (Pbk)
ISBN-10: 1-83998-197-0 (Pbk)

This title is also available as an ebook.

CONTENTS

PREFACE

Learning is a fundamental aspect of human existence. It forms one of the essential building blocks of growth and development and continues throughout life. We are constantly surrounded by opportunities to learn. Teaching is one of the key activities which shapes and contextualises our learning, and the choice to continue to formally learn beyond compulsory education is an important life choice, driven by a number of factors. It is a choice that an increasing number of young people and mature students take in the United Kingdom. The Higher Education (HE) sector is eager to demonstrate the benefits of continued post-compulsory education and the importance of a 'good' learning experience. The well-used term 'teaching excellence' is often employed as an articulation of the pedagogy, learning and learner experience, which come together to ensure effective teaching. There are inherent problematic issues in seeking to universally compare teaching and in finding ways to articulate and measure what can be diverse learning experiences.

This book explores the importance of teaching excellence and how this has risen to prominence in a changing landscape of HE where access to university education has been substantially increased. The book explores some of the factors which have shaped the provision of HE and the responses to the challenge of ensuring that students gain a quality education which provides a satisfactory return on their investment in attending university. Taking in the complexities of the differing perspectives on a university education from sector to student and acknowledging the experience of academics who seek to be excellent teachers, this book offers a guide to understanding the key mechanisms by which teaching is measured and evaluated and offers insights into some of the more contemporary innovative methodologies that can help to enhance teaching excellence.

Although offering a broad overview of teaching excellence in the United Kingdom, the book is of course not comprehensive in its coverage. The field of university metrics is extensive, multilayered and diverse; the coverage here will be sufficient to help readers understand the concept of 'teaching excellence' and the role of different players and lens through which it is viewed. The following overview of the teaching excellence terrain provides an introduction to inspire further reading and exploration of the areas included here.

Chapter 1

INTRODUCTION

Teaching excellence is of increasing importance within the Higher Education (HE) sector. In the current climate universities strive to demonstrate the value of their programmes and courses as they seek to attract students in a competitive marketplace. Within the context of this drive to attract students, institutions will readily state that they seek to pursue excellence in learning and teaching. However, it is less clear what constitutes 'excellence' when considered across a diverse sector with different traditions and practices relating to different disciplines. The problems associated with the ability to quantify and denote excellence in HE are compounded by the broad range of provision, the variation between institutions and the way in which universities position themselves and their offer to students. An unevenness exists across the sector in relation to teaching practices, class sizes and the philosophy of individual programmes and disciplines, and different contexts and approaches can exist even within a single university. There is no singular, identifiable culture for HE within the United Kingdom, and this makes comparisons between institutions potentially problematic.

Teaching is a complex practice affected by many factors: context, resources, learners, subject discipline, teacher experience, learning expectations and learning needs. It is also affected by the prevailing culture of the day; this includes, but is not limited to, the demographic of students and staff, the rise of social media, widening participation, funding constraints, digital technology and professional body requirements. These are but a few of the factors which impinge on the educational experience. Hence teaching is affected by multiple variables and is a dynamic, evolving practice that is impacted by a range of other elements and effects. Some of these are foreseeable and some are unanticipated but far-reaching, such as the Covid-19 pandemic of 2020 which altered the shape of HE suddenly and rapidly, creating a new 'normal' and a new set of comparisons. It is clear that HE does not and cannot operate in isolation to other factors. Developments and changes in one location can directly impact the sector globally. This is not just because students often travel to study but also because digital learning enables students to pursue courses remotely via e-learning across the world. This leads to a tendency for much broader comparisons between universities and their provision. Education and teaching are global activities, and this is reflected in world rankings and global league tables. Likewise, graduate skills are considered to be globally transferrable, attending not only to the demands of local employers but also to a fluid, dynamic and changing global workforce. Attendant on the acquisition of graduate skills is the need for students to be 'global citizens' equipped with not only demonstrable subject knowledge but also cultural awareness, resilience and a strong moral and ethical code.

Information is currency in the modern world, and information is everywhere. Information is readily available on curated sites and through social media, and this creates a particular challenge for educational institutions to successfully make the argument for taught courses and payment in exchange for knowledge. There is ongoing and lively debate on what it means to be 'educated' as opposed to being 'informed' or passively exposed to information through access to online information. It is clear that the HE sector needs to demarcate and articulate the added value that is inherent in providing education over enabling access to information. 'Education' as a term needs to be interrogated and examined in order to determine and agree what the hallmarks of 'good' teaching and learning are. Hence for teaching to be viewed as 'good', it needs to concern itself with the craft of applying knowledge, stimulating critical thinking, curating appropriate resources and working collectively. In other words, it is the practice of creating learning experiences in appropriate learning spaces which enables students to learn independently, confidently and effectively, at the same time being enabled to process relevant and credible information and work across disciplines.

Background

The context of HE in the United Kingdom has altered significantly in recent decades. There have been multiple drivers to changes within the sector. The Dearing Report (1997) recommended the introduction of a model of funding which ultimately led to the introduction of tuition fees paid by the student to the institution providing HE. This replaced a tapered grant system based on parental or personal income, which had been in place for many years and in which local authorities funded the education of their residents going to university to study. This alteration in the primary funding model led to a shift in the culture of HE and an accompanying change in the ways in which students view university education. The contemporary student is no longer just a recipient of HE but a customer making direct payments in exchange for educational provision. This cultural shift has altered the way in which universities see students, the way students view universities and also the ways in which universities see themselves. Customers are perceived as having greater agency and a greater capacity and inclination to critique the 'product' they are purchasing and to make comparisons with other 'product' offers. This has fed directly into both rhetoric and practice around the student experience and the perceptions of value for money.

Students often perceive their education in terms of lectures, and the value of education is often articulated in terms of how many lectures are scheduled in their course; in simplified terms this is a 'cost per lecture' model. The narrow focus of such a view overlooks the elements of teaching and learning which combine both formal and informal learning. It also ignores the plethora of learning opportunities and support which universities also provide for their students. In 2012, university fees for undergraduate programmes tripled in one year. Although the level has remained relatively constant in recent years, this sudden escalation in cost to the student resulted in an increasingly consumerist approach to HE. In the United Kingdom, a student studying in a three-year programme can be graduating with around £35,000 to £40,000 of student debt on average. Maybe, it could be argued that these costs are somewhat justified if the quality of the education the students were receiving was generally understood to be high and improving. However, many students may be disappointed to discover that their degree does not necessarily secure for them the type of job they anticipated they would initially have upon graduation. Students are also surprised or concerned at the length of time it will take them to pay off their student loans and costs associated with study.

This new model of funding HE led to a demand for tailored, personalised and accessible education, alongside the constant evaluation of student satisfaction with provision. Across the sector there was an emergent emphasis on trying to demonstrate that students were being offered a 'good' student experience. This in turn led to debates about whether a good student experience can be measured and compared between institutions in a hierarchical way, as occurs with league tables. It is difficult to compare 'like with like' when there are so many variables between institutions. The result was the introduction of the National Student Survey (NSS) in 2005, which follows an annual cycle (HEFCE, 2017a). The NSS, although central to evaluating student experience, was not the only measure to be introduced; it was accompanied by the introduction of specific research into identified elements of the student experience such as student contact hours (NUS, 2012). These drivers of a cultural shift in education have developed alongside the emergence of the Research Excellence Framework (REF) (HEFCE, 2017b), Knowledge Exchange Framework and Teaching Excellence Framework (TEF) (GovUK, 2017). TEF places a strong emphasis not only on teaching and learning but also on creating opportunities for students to gain the necessary skills for employment. Both the TEF and the REF encourage interdisciplinary education as part of the matrix criteria, emphasising opportunities beyond the learning and teaching on a specific programme, and highlight the importance of employability and enterprise in preparing students for the post-graduation workplace (Butcher et al., 2011).

The TEF is not without its critics. Interestingly, one of the key criticisms has been that the TEF has a tendency to separate 'teaching' from 'learning'. Some of the criteria which are related to student experience, for example, retention, may have multiple causes and may not have a direct causal link with teaching quality. However, the policy direction of travel is clear, and the scrutiny of teaching and learning is increasing, with bodies such as the Office for Students (OfS) (2018a) championing and monitoring student experience.

Alongside the introduction of tuition fees there have been other significant developments which have had an impact on teaching practices, not least the expansion of HE. This was a result of the Labour government policy in 1999 to enable 50 per cent of school leavers to receive a university education (BBC, 1999). The result was an extensive widening access agenda in post-compulsory education, designed to facilitate the increased level of HE participation. The impact has been a shift in the demographics of the student body leading to greater diversity within the sector and with increasing levels of participation from non-traditional backgrounds. This change is not evenly distributed across the sector. The post-1992 universities and former polytechnics have traditionally admitted a greater proportion of students from non-traditional backgrounds. This is not only due in part to the types of courses and programmes they offer but also complemented by the expertise in student support within this part of the sector and the links with industry and workforce development. There has also been an increase in the number of mature students returning to study. HE not only increasingly plays a part in skills development for the economy but also retains a role in social inclusion and social mobility, although it could be argued that at one time the achievement of a university degree carried more assurance of social mobility, although the entry and access to education might have been more limited.

Role of Funding for Teaching and Research in Higher Education Institutions

From 1986 to 2008 universities within the United Kingdom were subjected to the Research Assessment Exercise. This was undertaken every five years on behalf of the four main HE Funding Councils in order to assess and evaluate research quality. The rankings allocated to the units of assessment, which correlated to subject areas, informed the allocation of research funding to individual institutions. The units of assessment were evaluated by a subject-specialist peer review panel. In 2014 this mechanism was replaced by the REF.

The importance of the REF is again largely because within HE 'research quality' has traditionally been the most significant metric in terms of institutional prestige. This has a direct impact on league table rankings and in turn on the advancement and promotion opportunities for academic staff. Institutional prestige also has a direct impact on graduate opportunities for students. The emphasis on attracting research income has been paramount in the traditional research-intensive universities and has become the pattern and practice adopted by the postmodern universities too as they emulated existing institutions. It could be argued that this has maintained the focus on research and away from the importance of teaching, which is the key emphasis of many post-1992 institutions.

The REF is an impact assessment and is undertaken by the four HE funding bodies: Research England, Scottish Funding Council, Higher Education Funding Council for Wales and the Department of the Economy Northern Ireland. The stated aims of the REF are to provide accountability for public investment and therefore to ensure that resources are allocated appropriately. It is subject to criticisms that impact does not align with research quality and that there is too much focus on research outside of the university system. Research funding is a 'dual support mechanism' which comprises a funding grant and then money for specific projects. It is estimated that currently 66 per cent of income for research comes from the government.

By contrast less than 20 per cent of costs from teaching come from government grants and the rest comes from student fees. Non-EU student fees are unregulated and higher than for UK students (UUK, 2016). Universities with a TEF award are permitted to charge up to the higher maximum fee for 2019 UK entrants; this figure is less for Higher Education Institutions (HEIs) without a TEF award. The fees (tariff) figure is reassessed each academic year.

In 2019 the TEF was renamed the Teaching Excellence and Student Outcomes Framework to reflect that the measures for evaluation are deemed to be broader than teaching. The TEF comprises gold, silver and bronze levels for universities depending on evaluation of their submission. This change led to debate within the sector as to the extent to which the value of university education should be linked to measurement of postgraduate earning potential. This is particularly important given the myriad other factors that impact graduate employment, which include factors such as variance in earnings due to geographical location and the fact that mature and non-traditional students are less likely to move to other areas for work.

Incentives for Research Excellence Compared to Teaching Excellence

The existing funding model for HE means that, in short, the incentives for excellence in research can be measured, at least partly in financial terms, while the incentives for excellence in teaching have less of an established link to financial benefit to the institution. The higher recognition levels for teaching excellence will potentially have an impact on recruitment. This is partly due to the emphasis placed on league tables and rankings across the sector. However, the evidence is not necessarily conclusive in indicating that students are unduly influenced by TEF ratings in their choice of university. It is thought that a higher TEF rating may have more of an impact on the recommendations of teachers and career officers in encouraging potential students with university applications (Gov UK, 2019).

Within the sector incentives for Teaching Excellence persist and these include recognisable and identifiable status, teaching and student experience ratings, public perceptions and an indication of institutional priorities. It could be added that paying attention to an enhanced and improved career structure for academics who elect to remain in teaching and formalised measures to assist in developing and recognising their teaching practice could also play a part in incentivising teaching excellence.

Political Shifts in the UK Higher Education Policy

Teaching, and specifically teaching in HE, is a complex issue influenced by many variables. Teaching is both an art and a craft and there is an elusive element to understanding and capturing the essence of good teaching, which is difficult to ascertain by numerical measures and outcomes alone. While league tables can play a part in ranking provision, they overlook the issues which are difficult to measure and tend not to engage with the qualitative measures which contribute to positive teaching relationships and good teaching outcomes. These include areas such as building confidence in learners, overcoming imposter syndrome and facilitating and enabling the social changes which result from education. These areas are not as easy to evaluate, measure or compare as they are more qualitative by nature, but these more elusive elements are fundamentally essential to the successful progression and achievement for students from non-traditional backgrounds. Politically, league tables can only reflect a part of the story and lack the finesse required to uncover the social engagement and advancement parts of the hidden curriculum, particularly with regard to the changing demographics of students.

The changes within the student body are not solely down to government policy and the introduction of widening access measures in the 1990s and beyond. There are now a greater number of mature students in the HE system, particularly in vocational courses. Online provision has escalated, with 14 per cent of all students in the United Kingdom now classed as online learners (UUK, 2018) and an increasing proportion of flipped classroom learning on campus-based courses. Students are also more likely to be in paid work alongside their programmes of study, even if regarded as full-time students, as working alongside study has been normalised to enable students to meet the costs associated with study, which have risen in recent decades. There has also been an increase in provision which is shared with the workplace, such as higher levels of work placement provision, work-based learning elements, sandwich courses and degree apprenticeships. The current models of measurement, such as the NSS, encourage students to assess the quality of their experience based on campus experiences when the reality is that in many courses, much of their learning (and teaching) is provided by partners; one example of this is nursing programmes where 50 per cent of learning is in practice, but the NSS links all learning experiences to on-campus provision.

The background and experience of the learner are changing, the way in which learning is delivered is changing and the universities themselves are changing. The acceleration of change in learning experiences may also escalate due to recent experiences of closed campuses and online teaching due to the Covid-19 pandemic of 2020. Educational policy is struggling to evaluate and measure effectively and consistently the quality of both product and process in HE. Increasingly there is a need to pay attention to the work-based partners in contemporary HE and the impact their practices have on overall student experience. Although these partners directly shape the student experience through the workplace these educators are not employees of the host HEI. This makes quality assurance potentially problematic and hard to control without complex and time-consuming systems of investigation and remedial support. The logistics of workplace provision as part of a course can mean that unless there are effective and responsive systems to address student issues, it is difficult to remedy concerns in a short time scale.

In policy terms the sector has engaged with broader attempts to recognise, reward and quantify good teaching in HE. This has been not only through the increasing requirement for staff to demonstrate that they have had some teacher training by completing the PGCE or Academic Professional Apprenticeship but also via the recognition schemes for existing teachers in HE and also national awards. This reward and recognition began with the formation of the Institute for Learning and Teaching in HE (ILTHE), which was voluntary. Formed in 2008 the ILTHE encouraged all HE academic teaching staff to apply for recognition based on assessments of peer learning and references. In 2011 the Higher Education Academy (HEA) launched its UK Professional Standards Framework as a way of determining different categories of fellowship and recognition within the academy. This is discussed more fully in Chapter 3. With routes to recognition through direct application and dialogue routes and with a recognised and accredited scheme run by universities, this has become a widespread recognition rooted within the sector and now managed by Advance HE as the organisation which evolved from the HEA.

Within universities there has been enhanced acknowledgement of the need for a career structure for teaching and learning which mirrors the advancement and career paths for researchers. This has led to the development of Reader and Professorial posts for teaching excellence and Teaching Fellowship posts. This is an attempt in part to reflect on the skills inherent in good teaching as a scholarly endeavour. There is a long history of continued debate on the need to understand the craft of teaching and the endeavours engaged in its mastery (Roueche et al., 1995). Increasingly academics are also arguing that the competition driven by league tables, rankings and comparison is itself not conducive to the practice of good teaching. O'Leary and Wood (2018) make a strong case for a need for teaching excellence to be framed within the need for collaboration and not competition and the sharing of good practice.

Impacts of Teaching Excellence

The impact of the focus on teaching excellence has been to drive forward change within the sector at a number of junctures. The first of these is around the nature of teaching as a practice. The search for ways to measure and evaluate good teaching has begun to focus on the effective use of tools to support teaching rather than the individual skills of the teacher. This, partially at least, locates teaching excellence in the repertoire of resources available to the teacher and their ability to manage and deploy them. The 'good teacher' is not necessarily only conceived as a knowledgeable orator but rather also as a skilled technician curating and making available narrated, appropriate, navigable resources from a range of sources. The notion of teaching excellence is correlated with the investment within a university of teaching support, usually digital technology. In this model the institution has a greater role to play in creating and developing teachers as well as employing those with existing good teaching skills. This is reflected in the need for continued skills development and enhancement to keep abreast of developments in educational technology. Technology is not the only area to consider in the support for good teaching; the physical spaces for learning and the scope for creative approaches to learning, and the time for staff to engage with available resources, all become the measurable and visible elements of quantifying the pursuit of excellence in teaching.

Student Experience

It is the student who is repeatedly placed in the position to define and determine, through surveys and feedback, whether they perceive teaching to be excellent. While it is always good to ask the consumer to evaluate the package or produce they receive, there is also a danger that the real appreciation for 'good learning and teaching' is not always recognised or immediately attached to episodes of learning by learners. It is at best a rough measure of effective teaching as the usefulness of some learning may only become apparent later. Neither is success at assessment always the most useful evaluator of good teaching and learning. Sometimes what is assessed is not the most valuable element of learning and what is valuable cannot always easily be assessed, leaving a tension around the assessment process. The challenge is to measure and quantify something which by its very nature is intensely variable and which is experienced by different people in different ways. Measuring a positive student experience is an elusive and complex task, rendered more difficult by the variance within the consumers' group. Students may be inclined to unduly focus on the assessment and ignore the wider learning taking place. Evaluation forms tend to rely on capturing the experience of formal learning, such as lectures, seminars and materials, and resources available via virtual learning environment. However, this may overlook the informal learning which takes place through networks, social connections, extracurricular activities and the broader offerings of non-subject-specific lectures and learning opportunities which are also a part of HE experience. As already mentioned, evaluations such as the NSS focus on HE provisions that may be reliant on work-based provision from stakeholders, which may be subject to additional pressures and effects. An example of this would be the NHS as an educational placement provider during the Covid-19 pandemic, the pressures on the service potentially having an impact on student experience while on placement.

Many universities have sought to pay greater attention to the mechanisms by which the 'student voice' can be readily heard in relation to the student experience. This may be through closer involvement with the Students' Union, Student Representatives and formal structures to gather this feedback, or it can be via more informal means such as feedback boards where any student can anonymously raise issues for consideration by their school or department. There are also other ways in which student experience can be expressed or captured; use of co-creation of resources with students and academic staff is another way in which the student voice can influence and shape educational provision, and additionally peer-based systems such as PASS (Peer Assisted Study Scheme) and mentoring schemes enable and facilitate students to influence educational delivery.

The student experience is also contextualised by their expectations of HE and the existing skills, confidence and knowledge they bring to their university education. There has been a move towards considering the 'value' added by an educational experience, which is an attempt to take into account the fact that students begin with different qualifications and advantages and do not all commence HE study at the same place. For HE to have a meaningful value-added measure it would require measurements of student ability at the entry point and end point of their university course that are comparable across the sector. For home students this entry point measure could be the equivalent Universities and Colleges Admissions Service (UCAS) points score. But it is difficult to accurately quantify the value added by HE programmes. There is always an element of externality to assessment criteria and student achievement via the use of External Examiners and subject benchmarking, yet it is still difficult to compare performance in relation to other courses and programmes within a subject area, as they may have differing content and different assessment modes. Even within professional courses there has been an increasing reluctance for degrees to incorporate a national final standard examination, relying on individual universities to ensure that the criteria are met through their own assessment processes. There is a remarkable degree of complexity in attempting to unpick and separate the different factors which lead to academic success and what constitutes demonstrable and comparable 'value' in these contexts. It is easier to ignore nuance of social, psychological and economic experience and instead focus on only assessment outcomes. There is, therefore, a tendency to default to measuring what can be readily measured.

Academic Progression

The pursuit of excellence in teaching has resulted in a new direction emerging in respect of academic careers. It is now no longer necessary to leave teaching behind and prioritise research in order to progress. The creation of new career structures, together with rewards and awards for teaching excellence, is changing the landscape for academics with a greater emphasis on skills development. This is accompanied by an increasing recognition of the value of pedagogic research and scholarship of learning and teaching. There is a stronger imperative for academics who focus on teaching to evaluate and research their pedagogic practice in order to contribute to a growing body of knowledge on the practice of teaching and the nature of learning.

One of the greatest impacts of the move towards recognition and reward of teaching excellence at the national, sector, institutional and career levels has been a focus on the narrative of excellence and the opening up of the debate around what constitutes good teaching and whether this is multiple or singular. The narrative of teaching excellence has caused HE to redefine itself and to reconfigure what learning means in an information age and how it can best be effectively accomplished.

Conclusions

This chapter has provided an overview of how teaching excellence may be viewed from multiple standpoints. These include the political evolution of HE which has transitioned for a contained and small minority of the population attending university as part of an academic elite to the broadening of entry to HE through the widening participation agenda. This places an emphasis on quality assurance and a desire to ensure that although university education may have become more accessible, it has not been universally met with a decline in academic standards of graduates and an associated focus on graduate outcomes. It is also accompanied by comparisons, league tables and evaluations of perceived quality. A different lens by which to view teaching excellence involves student experience and the increasing focus on students as 'consumers' and customers who pay for and receive a service. The focus here is on satisfaction and evaluation as to whether the educational experience provided value for money. Yet another viewpoint that is offered is the potential separation of teaching and research careers, in which academics with a teaching role seek recognition and reward, with a career structure which supports the development and achievement of teaching excellence. This not only places 'teaching excellence' at the centre of student experience but also articulates it as a career 'standard' for academic teaching staff. These different perspectives and facets intersect with the quantifying, articulating and experiencing of what is meant by 'teaching excellence'.

Chapter 2

IMPORTANCE OF TEACHING EXCELLENCE: WHAT MATTERS?

Introduction

'Teaching excellence' is not a simple concept and, as a concept, lacks precision. (Elton, 1998, 3).

While excellence is often perceived as a concept linked with individual virtue or quality, it is also referred to as an organisational characteristic by which universities recognise a vertical stratification which promotes exceptionality (Tavaras, 2014).

Excellence in Higher Education (HE) has more often become *the* expectation of all. 'Teaching Excellence' in particular is the definition of how we teach, how students learn and how we justify value to students and stakeholders. An internet search of HE providers suggests that many promote themselves as offering excellent teaching. The UK regulator for HE, the Office for Students (OfS), and the UK professional standards framework both articulate minimum expectations for teaching excellence. Inherent in these definitions is that excellence is the expectation, not a definition of exceptionality. For the purpose of this chapter the concept of excellence is therefore that of an expected customer service standard: one which underpins our professionalism, our values and our sense of success.

This chapter explores those aspects that define teaching excellence in the UK HE sector. It recognises the importance of teaching excellence to learners, professionals, the sector and HE policy agendas. In conclusion it recognises how a focus on teaching excellence has changed behaviours within the sector.

Student Numbers Entering HE

The number of students going into HE in the United Kingdom has been growing steadily since the mid-1990s. This was a stated objective of

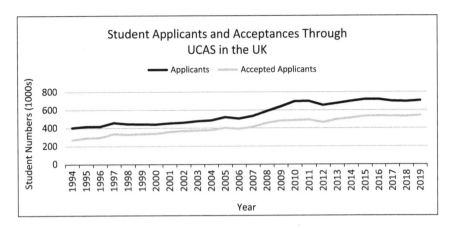

Figure 1 Graph showing the rising trend in student numbers entering HE in the United Kingdom.

government policy back in 1999 when the then Prime Minister Tony Blair made a pledge that 50 per cent of all young people should be in HE by the year 2010. Although this objective was not reached fully by the 2010 deadline, it did reach around 49 per cent by the year 2017 (Adams, 2017).

Figure 1 summarises trends over a 25-year period since the Universities and Colleges Admissions Service (UCAS[1]) was created following the reform of the sector in the early 1990s. It is clearly observed that student application numbers have been steadily rising since the mid-1990s except for the years 2006 and 2012 when there were dips corresponding to the introduction of variable fees and a rise in fees to £9,000 per year respectively.

With more and more students entering HE came a radical shift in the funding model for students going to university. Government policy reforms deemed that the state could no longer sustain funding for these higher number of students in HE and so student fees and subsequently student loans were introduced. Home students currently pay £9,250 in fees per year; in light of this the government wants to hold universities to account for the quality of teaching and student outcomes and has introduced the Teaching Excellence Framework (TEF) to ensure that students are getting value for their money.

---

1. A UK-based organisation whose main role is to operate the student application process for British universities.

What Is Teaching Excellence?

The policy environment and the review of the TEF

Within the UK HE environment, the Teaching Excellence and Student Outcomes Framework (TEF[2]) has become a well-rehearsed definition of teaching excellence. The pre-eminence of this definition comes from the broad engagement of contemporary experts and practitioners in debating and drafting the definition. The standard is 'owned' by the regulatory body (the OfS) leading to the sector having little alternative but to base success on being able to articulate actions and outcomes against this framework.

The TEF has been subject to an independent review. Published in 2021, an independent review (Department for Education, 2021d) recognises the positive impact of the TEF, noting the greater focus and engagement on teaching and learning, teaching quality and student engagement and how the framework has ensured that teaching quality is higher on the agenda of governing bodies. Despite these benefits there are 'costs and unintended consequences': staff time and the administrative burden is high, poor outcomes have impacted on staff morale and reputational damage. The review suggests that, as a result of TEF, the sector is more competitive and less cooperative. There are also examples of the sector becoming more risk-averse.

The review nevertheless makes a number of recommendations to enhance the TEF. The government response ((Department for Education, 2021b) agrees in principle, yet challenges some of the recommendations, thereby paving the way for a different kind of exercise. At the time of writing, it appears that a TEF will remain with the purpose to identify excellence and encourage enhancement. This will be underpinned by transparent, relevant, robust principles, with a sense of proportionality to minimise the administrative burden on providers. It is likely to be a periodic exercise (every four or five years) with a rating system applied to each of the four aspects of the framework and as an overall provider rating.

The aspects are grouped around Education Experience comprising (i) Teaching and Learning Environment and (ii) Student Academic Experience; Educational Outcomes comprising (iii) Educational Gains and (iv) Graduate Outcomes. Each aspect will be assessed against nationally comparable metrics, a provider submission and a student submission. It is worth observing that the

---

2. At the time of writing the TEF is under review with an expectation that the framework will remain in some form.

measure of 'educational gain' remains undefined, with suggestion that it will be for the provider to determine its own measure of educational gain.

The Pearce report recommended a rating system, comprising four judgements ranging from 'meets UK quality requirements' to 'outstanding'. The government response nevertheless suggests that the lowest category should signify that providers are failing to show sufficiency of excellence (Department for Education, 2021b).

As the final details of the new TEF are being developed it is evident that policy makers are seeking to embed TEF further into the regulatory framework for HE in the United Kingdom, thereby requiring providers to continue to demonstrate value to students. The inclusion of a measure to signify insufficiency has the potential to make the TEF a higher stakes exercise.

While the TEF has proved that all providers are able to articulate their version of teaching excellence against a common framework, there remain many who question the value of such an exercise. Institutions regularly debate the validity of data used to inform decisions. Common critique focuses around cries of 'we are different' or suggestions that the National Students' Survey (NSS) or employability data sets are not accurate reflections of their context.

The National Union of Students (NUS) has boldly stated, 'The TEF doesn't actually measure Teaching Excellence.' They go on to inform their members that the government will be judging teaching quality based on a written submission by the university and three core measures:[3] 'These are unreliable measures and influenced by many factors such as the university's location and socio-economic status – not to mention the amount of freebies and gimmicks universities offer to encourage more positive ratings in the NSS' (NUS, 2017).

The National Students' Survey

The reference to the NSS is an interesting one. If we are to define teaching excellence, surely this should be as defined and judged by the recipient, the student. To take the analogy of a cake, an excellent cake would be one that looks and tastes good, not necessarily that which can be described as having the best ingredients and recipe.

The NSS is an annual survey of students which asks questions about their experience (Table 1). The survey delivers comparable data at institution, subject or course level. It informs the TEF and it provides students with benchmarks by which to compare the offer from different providers. Those who debate its value note that, despite built-in safeguards, it is widely recognised

---

3. TEF core measures are defined as three aspects of quality: teaching quality, learning environment, and student outcomes and learning gain.

Table 1 NSS 2020 Core Questions

The teaching on my course

1. Staff are good at explaining things.
2. Staff have made the subject interesting.
3. The course is intellectually stimulating.
4. My course has challenged me to achieve my best work. Learning opportunities

Learning opportunities

5. My course has provided me with opportunities to explore ideas or concepts in depth.
6. My course has provided me with opportunities to bring information and ideas together from different topics.
7. My course has provided me with opportunities to apply what I have learnt.

Assessment and feedback

8. The criteria used in marking have been clear in advance.
9. Marking and assessment has been fair.
10. Feedback on my work has been timely.
11. I have received helpful comments on my work. Academic support

Academic support

12. I have been able to contact staff when I needed to.
13. I have received sufficient advice and guidance in relation to my course.
14. Good advice was available when I needed to make study choices on my course.

Organisation and management

15. The course is well organised and is running smoothly.
16. The timetable works efficiently for me.
17. Any changes in the course or teaching have been communicated effectively.

Learning resources

18. The IT resources and facilities provided have supported my learning well.
19. The library resources (e.g. books, online services and learning spaces) have supported my learning well.
20. I have been able to access course-specific resources (e.g. equipment, facilities, software, collections) when I needed to.

Learning community

21. I feel part of a community of staff and students.
22. I have had the right opportunities to work with other students as part of my course.

Student voice

23. I have had the right opportunities to provide feedback on my course.
24. Staff value students' views and opinions about the course.
25. It is clear how students' feedback on the course has been acted on.
26. The students' union (association or guild) effectively represents students' academic interests.
27. Overall, I am satisfied with the quality of the course.
28. Looking back on the experience, are there any particularly positive or negative aspects you would like to highlight?

Note: At the time of writing the NSS is under review.

that negative NSS scores can influence the value of the degree being attained by those who give that score. Different learners value their learning differently. To follow the cake analogy above, not everyone will like the same cake; it is a question of taste.

Another excellent source of student feedback is the annual Student Academic Experience Survey which since 2006 has provided a longitudinal view of the student experience, including perception of teaching quality. It is interesting to note the importance given to the perception of teaching staff; the 2020 survey recognises how the characteristics of teaching staff can help contribute to more positive levels of well-being and the importance of teaching staff helping students explore their own areas of weakness by regularly initiating debates and discussion (Neves and Hewitt, 2020).

While the intrinsic value of the TEF and NSS can be debated, both act as tools to monitor performance and demonstrate the public value of HE. The policy environment has made this a necessity. The Teaching and Higher Education Act 1998 enabled universities to charge tuition fees and made provision for the introduction of student loans. The Higher Education and Research Act 2017 created the new regulatory framework for HE, with the purpose to increase competition and student choice, ensure students receive value for money and strengthen the research sector. As a result, the sector's definition of teaching excellence is increasingly focused on the value of HE.

The value of HE

The definition of value is contested. To continue the cake analogy, value can be understood in relation to money; did I get what I paid for? Value may however be a more emotional sentiment; it felt good. It may represent a personal priority or need; the cake tasted nice and it filled me up, or didn't add too many calories. From an education policy perspective, value could be a definition of how the education meets a policy agenda, for example, to enable social mobility, to ensure access and participation, or to boost highly skilled employment or economic stability. HE can do all of these things and therefore our personal accountability to consider how we provide value is important. Teaching excellence must include our responsibility to add value, through cost effectiveness, inclusivity and employability.

The OfS (2018b) asked students what value for money meant to them, whether or not they were receiving it and what could be done to improve it. The findings demonstrate that value for money means different things to different students and may shift over time. Nevertheless, the quality of teaching, assessment and feedback are important to over 90 per cent of respondents,

Table 2 League table metrics (2018)

Guardian	The Times & Sunday Times	Complete University Guide
Entry qualifications	Entry qualifications	Entry qualifications
Student satisfaction	Student satisfaction	Student satisfaction
• Satisfied overall	• Student experience	Student:staff ratio
• Satisfied with teaching	• Teaching quality	Completion
• Satisfied with feedback	Student:staff ratio	Degree classifications
Student:staff ratio	Completion	Graduate careers
Value-added score	Degree classifications	Research quality
Graduate careers	Graduate careers	Research intensity
Spend per student	Research quality	Academic services spend per student
	Services and facilities spend per student	Facilities spend per student

Source: Turnbull (2018, p. 17).

as are library and IT services. The OfS (2019) additionally recognises how 'providers must also support their students, from admission through to completion, so that they succeed in and benefit from higher education'.

League tables

Published league tables are often used as tools to promote value; providers elect to reference those tables and rankings which are of most benefit to attracting learners or informing stakeholders. The league tables are also used by Executive teams to define key performance metrics and benchmark performance. In the United Kingdom there are three main tables. The full list of metrics used is illustrated in Table 2 and refers to the 2018 versions. The detail of the data and calculations used within each of the different university league tables varies both from table to table and over time; methodologies will continue to evolve over time (Turnbull, 2018).

Turnbull notes that much of the essential value of HE is difficult to quantify, noting that as there are no agreed standards against which providers can be measured and academic peer review is resource intensive, league table compilers therefore use proxies to represent the unmeasured (or unmeasurable). The Guardian league table is the only one to include a value-added score. This aims to measure 'distance travelled' between entry and graduation. This benefits those providers offering a lower entry tariff and enabling learners to achieve higher degree outcomes (first or upper-second-class degree).

Inclusivity

To demonstrate value is to enable anyone with potential to achieve or exceed their ambition. Direct attention to this area of practice is usually articulated through 'inclusive learning' and 'access and participation' activities.

Access and participation recognises how the institution enables access to HE and works to eliminate attainment gaps between underrepresented groups and their peers through a focus on success (non-continuation and attainment) and progression to employment or further study. Institutions must have an approved Access and Participation Plan (APP) as a condition of OfS regulation. The plans include the approved student fee, based on the commitments made within the plan. Each APP sets out how the provider will improve equality of opportunity as the student enters and progresses through and beyond their education experience. The plan outlines the institution's performance in relation to the gaps between underrepresented groups and their peers, and progress over time in closing the gaps, considered in relation to both the institution's own student population and their role in the national picture as evidenced against national and local quantitative and qualitative data sets.

As educators our responsibility is to provide an inclusive learning environment; 'teachers need to be equipped with appropriate competences for addressing the diverse needs and preferences of their students and providing them with equal educational opportunities' (Baldiris Navarro et al., 2016, 25). Frameworks have been developed to support educators in this endeavour, one of the most familiar being Universal Design for Learning (UDL).

Adapted from concepts developed in relation to the built environment UDL, developed by the Centre for Applied Special Technology (CAST), is a framework to support teachers as they create engaging and accessible learning and assessment. The three principles are:

- *Representation*: recognises that learners differ in the ways that they perceive and comprehend information that is presented to them. The teacher should present educational resources in different ways: oral, print, video, pictures or diagrams, thereby providing options for different representations.
- *Action and Expression*: allows learners to demonstrate what they have learnt in different ways. The traditional essay or timed examination can be daunting for many; educators increasingly provide choice of assessment types or greater variety of assessment modes including projects, oral presentations, practical demonstrations or group activity.
- *Engagement*: recognises that some learners prefer to work alone, while others like to work with their peers. There is not one means of engagement that will be optimal for all learners in all contexts; teachers should consider

classroom strategies that empower their learners and draw them into the learning by providing choices, reducing anxiety and rewarding effort (Baldiris Navarro et al., 2016).

Advance HE recognises how reducing attainment gaps has been the subject of much interest and research. There is no quick or single solution to tackling inequalities that are deeply entrenched. Actions will take time to have impact and should be developed in the context of the culture of the institution and supported by a commitment to long-term resource. Students should be partners. Importantly 'action needs to focus on institutional barriers and inequalities, rather than "improving" or "fixing" the student. Traditionally the language of the attainment gap has focused on students' underachievement or lack of attainment, whereas it should focus on the institutional culture, curriculum and pedagogy' (Advance HE, 2020).

While focused on the needs of students with disability, Layer (2017, 19) notes some practical changes that can make a real difference to student outcomes:

- House all teaching materials on the virtual learning environment in such a way that students can access them when they are needed, before or after formal teaching.
- Improve the accessibility of all materials provided (even if just with the right sub-headings or an appropriate use of font).
- Ensure reading lists are focussed and up to date.
- Allow or facilitate the recording of teaching.
- Use plain English and clear presentation in lectures.
- Pre-select diverse learning groups.
- Diversify the range of learning opportunities, approaches and assessment methods.
- Regard students as learning partners.

Further to this universities have implemented policy change which demonstrates their commitment to widening access. By way of example this includes the Gypsy, Traveller, Roma, Showman and Boater (GTRSB) into Higher Education Pledge. Developed by Buckinghamshire New University the pledge consists of a firm commitment by a University, College or Educational Institution to undertake certain steps to support GTRSB students into and within HE. It is designed to support best practice in ensuring monitoring of data; inclusive pedagogy and representation in the academy; and the development of widening participation practice to support GTRSB students and potential students. Other policies include bursaries and funding, access policies and alignment with institution-wide race equality activities.

Employability

Most students entering university do so to enhance their career prospects. The premise of the English student loan policy is that students will enter into higher paid graduate-level employment, and only once they do so will they repay the cost of their HE. In looking to measure student value, graduate earnings are used as a metric of success. An extrapolation of this logic leads to the conclusion that better teaching leads to higher salaries and therefore student success and added value.

This analysis is contested on the basis of students not always being motivated by earnings. Students and recent graduates say that they decided to go to university for a broad range of reasons, including their interest in their chosen degree subject (56 per cent), enjoying studying and learning (48 per cent) and as a first step in building a career (50 per cent). Around 84 per cent agreed that their future salary was not the only factor they considered when deciding to go to university (Universities UK, 2019). Indeed, many important graduate-level public sector or creative industry careers are equally of importance to the national economy but do not levy high salaries. Male economics graduates can expect to earn a premium of £14,000 over their creative peers. The top 10 per cent of the highest-paid male medical graduates earn more than £84,700 a year, and for women that figure is £68,800. For creative arts graduates, the highest earners are paid upwards of £35,300 (for women) and £37,400 (for men) (Minsky, 2016). All disciplines should be as important to the mission and purpose of HE providers; the data used to record earnings is not an accurate reflection of value or takes account of other factors that may determine earning potential (e.g. prior attainment, parental background or social class) (Carrington, 2019).

Regardless of these critiques there is a logic for excellent teaching to lead to high-skilled employment. The moral imperative is to enable students to secure employment and to demonstrate their professional competence at a graduate level. This is evidenced by the inclusion of employability metrics within the TEF.

University/employer partnerships offer multiple benefits through the knowledge exchange, research and civic duties inherent in the priorities outlined in many university strategies. These relationships are also used to good effect in enhancing the learning experience. Live project briefs, placement opportunities, mentoring and visiting speakers are now the staple in most undergraduate education. Despite this just 66 per cent of working age graduates are in high-skilled employment (Department for Education, 2020).

The UK Government's Skills for Jobs White Paper (January 2021) recognises the important role universities can play in enabling skilled employment. This is underpinned by qualification and funding structures which ensure that

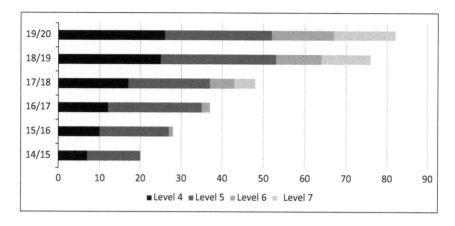

Figure 2 Higher level apprenticeship starts 2014/15 to 2019/20 (thousands).

Source: DfE Apprenticeships and Traineeships data.

employers and education providers are equally committed to both employment and skills development. The White Paper talks of transforming the post-16 skills agenda, encouraging more people to take higher technical education courses and get high-skilled work (Department for Education, 2021f).

Higher and Degree Apprenticeships

Higher and Degree Apprenticeships have for some time provided an alternative pathway to employment for university learners and further opportunities are expected. The post-18 education and funding review (Department for Education, 2021e) outlines plans to rebalance technical and academic education which will 'put an end to the illusion that a degree is the only route to success and a good job, and that further and technical education is the second-class option. Instead, they will supercharge further and technical education, realigning the whole system around the needs of employers, so that people are trained for the skills gaps that exist now, and in the future' (Williamson, 2021).

The growth of higher level (levels 4 to 7) apprenticeships demonstrates that many employers are seeking higher level skills (Figure 2) (Department for Education, 2021a).

Apprenticeship funding is contingent on the shared commitment to learner success demonstrated by both the provider and the employer. Additionally, the underpinning quality regime requires the education provider to demonstrate how each learner is provided with every opportunity to progress in their learning, how functional skills are developed and how the learning meets the national standards as set in the apprenticeship standard.

In July 2020, the government published plans for the future of higher technical education (Department for Education, 2021c). This includes new national qualifications linked to national occupational standards to ensure that courses and providers are delivering qualifications which meet the needs of employers and recognised quality standards. It is proposed that these will, in part, be delivered through further investment in Institutes of Technology (IoTs). IoTs are collaborations between further education, universities and employers. They have a specific focus on the delivery of level 4 and 5 technical education in STEM subjects such as engineering, construction and digital.

Through the national reform agendas outlined above universities and HE providers have clear frameworks through which to ensure learning meets the needs of employers and leads to employment for graduates. With this comes the removal of the autonomy that providers have previously had in defining the curriculum content.

This is of course not completely new. Many professional bodies require learners to demonstrate competence at a minimum standard, for example, in nursing, medicine, law, surveying or engineering. Many HE courses are accredited to the relevant professional standards, thereby enabling graduate-level membership.

The Professional Environment

The UK HE sector has worked hard to professionalise the HE teaching role. My own academic role has been defined in this way. In my early years of teaching (the late 1990s) I completed my PGCert in Teaching and Learning in Higher Education. To achieve a teaching qualification was unusual at that time. Roll on 20 years and the sector is afforded well-respected professional standards articulated in the UK Professional Standards Framework for Teaching and Supporting Learning (UKPSF). Indeed, a number of HE providers mandate achievement of a relevant teaching qualification or an 'Academic Apprenticeship' as part of probation in teaching roles.

The Higher Education Academy (HEA) (now Advance HE) was formed with the mission 'to support the higher education community in order to enhance the quality and impact of learning and teaching' (HEA Strategic Plan 2012–2016). As guardians of the UKPSF professional framework this organisation has done much to define the excellent teacher and to embed way of defining teaching excellence.

Achievement against this Advance HE framework (see Chapter 3) is a recognised tool to acknowledge excellent teachers and often used as a condition for recruitment, progression, and reward and recognition. The three dimensions of the framework incorporate the *Activity* undertaken, the *Core Knowledge* required to undertake that activity and the *Professional Values* demonstrated.

This framework has become a powerful barometer, both directly and indirectly, in informing and directing how the sector views teaching excellence. At an *individual level* it provides the scaffold for personal professional development and career transition. At an *organisational level* it provides a defensible concept on which to base staff performance expectations, development programmes, career progression and reward. At the *national level* it provides sector assurance of teaching competence.

Students are our customers. Many universities have implemented student-led teaching awards which enable learners to nominate those who demonstrate teaching excellence. An analysis of nominations at Edinburgh University (Lubicz-Nawrocka and Bunting, 2019) identifies four key themes of student conceptualisations of teaching excellence: (i) concerted visible effort; (ii) commitment to engaging students, (iii) breaking down student–teacher barriers, (iv) stability of support. A couple of years ago I asked a regular recipient of a student-led teaching award for best lecturer to explain his magic. He summarised this: 'I care about my students!' He explained how he applies all four elements as concluded in the Edinburgh study.

The evidence above outlines the importance that learners give to the professional values element of the framework, particularly respecting individual learners and promoting participation and equality of opportunity.

Teaching excellence as a statement of our professionalism as educators is powerful. The definition has moved away from 'happy sheet' module evaluations to something deeper: something which acknowledges the complexity of the role. Teaching excellence is not just about taste, it is about the tools we have and how we use them. Back to the cake analogy – consumers judge my cake by its taste, but as a professional baker I know how to choose the right ingredients in the right quantity and mix and bake them to perfection. This is the framework that I judge myself against. I only know that I have got this right if the final cake has risen to perfection and tastes good to those who consume it. I craft my art by working through new techniques, seeking feedback and always seeking to improve. From the perspective of the practitioner teaching is a craft.

Conclusions

This narrative provides an overview of the contemporary context for defining and understanding teaching excellence. It acknowledges well-intended approaches embedded in legislation, policy and cultural norms. While there are those who contest the approaches and definitions some common elements are embedded. Excellent teaching is shorthand for the expected norm; excellent teaching welcomes everyone regardless of background and provides an equality of opportunity to be successful; excellent teaching enables learners to meet their aspirations and progress to employment or further study.

It is not surprising that we find dissatisfaction or frustration in some sectors of our community; policy interventions rarely please all those affected by them. They are important. These definitions and priorities for teaching excellence influence overall institutional success and define the criteria by which our excellence is assessed, monitored and rewarded. These principles guide our governing bodies and executives in their priorities and decision-making.

These definitions nevertheless risk missing a sense of fun or enjoyment as a result of learning. We risk baking a cake, using the best ingredients, mixed with professionalism and care, but it is not being attractive to the recipient; does it taste right? Does it look like I expected?

These frameworks and definitions can lead us to matter about what is measured. In a regulated environment this can be inevitable but can also lead to a narrowing of ambition and understanding, along with a feeling of losing autonomy or professional leadership.

From a practitioner perspective we should measure what matters. We will get to the same place but will achieve this with a greater sense of ownership, professional autonomy and engagement with the learners and the policy agendas.

Effective teaching has the biggest influence on student outcomes. Teachers impact student achievement, engagement and motivation for learning. How we interact with students is vital. We have four key responsibilities for improving practice: building practice excellence, curriculum planning and assessment, evidence-based high-impact teaching strategies and evaluating the impact of teaching.

We are all responsible and accountable for teaching excellence. We demonstrate this through our reflective practice, our professionalism and our engagement with institutional priorities and partnership with our students. We are craft bakers, making cakes using the best ingredients, mixed to perfection, taking account of the needs of our customers. Our cakes look and taste great to both the novice and the expert consumer.

Chapter 3

WHAT CONSTITUTES TEACHING EXCELLENCE?

Best Measures of Teaching Excellence

Implementation of the teaching excellence framework

There are now more students entering Higher Education (HE) in the United Kingdom than ever before. HE is no longer limited just to the privilege of the elite few but where one in three school leavers continue to study at university level (Kershaw, 2019). With the changes in the early 1990s that created the post-1992 modern universities, the number of institutions with the title 'university' has also increased dramatically to now well over one hundred in the United Kingdom.

In many countries across the world the cost of HE is expensive with students having acquired a huge debt by the end of their programme that ultimately must be repaid. In the United States, for instance, typically, one year in a private university can cost around $30,000 when all costs are accounted for. In the United Kingdom, student debts are now averaging around £35,000 which is expected to be paid back but only when graduates are earning above a certain threshold amount and they do not have to make any repayments if they are out of work or their income goes below the threshold level.

In the United Kingdom, the government, as part of its reforms of the HE sector, placed a greater emphasis on giving students more choices about their options for HE. Where previously there was a general lack of information for students regarding the quality of teaching within an institution, students were not able to make informed choices regarding the suitability of a university for their needs, now information is available in the form of league tables and Teaching Excellence Framework (TEF) awards.

Variability related to teaching activities within different institutions is high and has meant that some students only receive a few hours of actual teaching contact time on a weekly basis compared to other students that have a significantly higher number of hours of contact per week while studying the same course in another location. Students entering HE need to make important decisions regarding what and where to study.

The UK government considers that the best way these choices can be made by students is to have a framework that can gather information which measures teaching in the broadest possible way. As previously discussed, this is comparable to the Research Excellence Framework (REF). To give students information on where the best provision can be found and to improve teaching quality at all Higher Education Institutions (HEIs) the TEF was introduced. Clearly, it is of the utmost importance that academic staff involved in teaching and assessment are professionally qualified in their specialist subjects and have a good understanding of the range of pedagogy associated with teaching and learning. If teaching excellence is seen as being especially important to the value of education, then academic staff must have a high level of competence in these areas. HEIs can and must make requirements to ensure that all teaching academics are able to demonstrate these teaching qualities through successful completion of relevant courses and recognition of teaching skills such as becoming at a minimum 'fellows' of Advance HE.

UK Professional Standards Framework

The UK Professional Standards Framework (UKPSF) was originally developed in the United Kingdom but now has an international base all over the world, with its main objective to support teaching and learning development in HEIs. Working with individuals and HEIs, Advance HE aims to provide students with an excellent learning experience (Advance HE, 2011b).

The Professional Standards Framework (PSF) identifies those elements that comprise successful teaching and learning. These elements are identified through what is known as the Dimensions of Professional Practice and fall into three main categories as follows:

(i)   Areas of Activity – Academics and those who support learning
(ii)   Core Knowledge – Subject and pedagogic knowledge required to deliver the activities at an appropriate level
(iii) Professional Values – Characteristics that can be demonstrated by those performing the activities

There are five components that comprise the 'Area of Activity, six components for the Core Knowledge and four components in the Professional Values that make up the Dimensions of Professional Practice'. These can be seen in Figure 3 (Advance HE, 2011b).

Figure 3 The UKPSF Dimensions of the Framework (Advance HE).

As can be seen from Figure 3, there are 15 essential components in the UKPSF Dimensions of Framework that all teaching staff must be able to carry out, have knowledge of and be practising a set of principle values that are central to the teaching profession.

Academic staff should be able to demonstrate the different components in their teaching practice and gain recognition through the Advance HE as a 'Fellow' giving them national as well as international teaching status.

Table 3 gives a summary of the four different categories of Fellowship that can be awarded based on evidence provided of one's personal professional practice

Table 3 The different categories of Fellowship within the Advance HE

Fellowship Category	Description
Associate Fellow (AFHEA)	• Carry out some teaching/learning support work
	• Understand specific aspects of effective teaching/learning methods
Fellow (FHEA)	• Show effectiveness in more substantive teaching and/or support learning
	• Broader understanding of effective teaching and/or learning pedagogies
Senior Fellow (SFHEA)	• A thorough understanding of effective pedagogies to teaching and/or learning support
	• Able to demonstrate impact and influence on other colleagues in relation to effective teaching and/or learning
Principal Fellow (PFHEA)	• Demonstrate a sustained record of a wide-ranging and effective strategic leadership in academic practice and development associated with teaching and learning

(Advance HE, 2011a). HEIs that are emphasising excellence in teaching by supporting their staff with the necessary time and resources in enabling them to achieve at a minimum 'Fellow' status of the Advance HE will therefore in turn be helping to enhance the teaching and learning experience of their students.

How Do Teachers Become Effective at Teaching?

Most teaching staff will agree that there are many attributes required for effective teaching in addition to having expert knowledge of the subject area. This expertise in subject knowledge has generally been shown through achieving higher degrees and publications in quality peer-reviewed journals which then may result in academic appointments. However, regarding their teaching expertise, there is generally extraordinarily little evidence to demonstrate their effectiveness as good teachers. There may be individuals that have gained some form of teacher training qualification such as a PGCE certificate, but this is not always an essential prerequisite for employment within HEIs. Clearly there may be many ways to teach effectively, but most academics will agree that there are common qualities that make teachers effective. Being well-prepared, showing enthusiasm, recognising that students are not all the same and therefore learn in different ways, and the ability of the teacher to reflect constantly on their own teaching practice to see if the students are really learning are just some of the essential qualities required. There is also the need for a good understanding of the theories of learning and teaching and being able to apply them in context. It is also important to understand that teaching becomes most effective when the students are motivated with the desire to learn more about the subject matter inside and even outside of the classroom or the learning space.

An important role of any effective teacher is the ability to explain complicated concepts in ways that are simple and easy for students to understand. This may require reviewing prior basic concepts before embarking on the more advanced material. Consideration then needs to be given of how best these complex ideas can be explained using a range of different methods such as discussions and making use of visual aids as deemed necessary.

For teachers to be more effective practitioners, it is important for them to be aware of and have knowledge of the different learning styles, namely Active and Passive Learning. For a long time, there has been an awareness among teaching professionals and academics that students who are lectured to by the teacher and essentially remain passive only manage to retain an exceedingly small proportion of the material presented to them in the classroom compared to those actively engaging in tasks that require them to use their knowledge base. Therefore, to maximise the student learning experience so that they can gain a much more in-depth understanding of the material and the subject matter, tutorials, lectures and classes need to be complemented by active learning; that is, having a range of activities which support the theoretical basis of their studies such as group activities, solving real-world problems and question and answer sessions.

The Teaching Profession requires engagement with a series of processes in which the teacher is continually involved; these include the planning of sessions, delivery, evaluation and reflection. Having considered effective planning and delivery, what must also be considered carefully is the process of evaluation and revision of strategies being used. Without the mechanism for feedback such as assessments or student feedback it becomes exceedingly difficult for the teacher to assess the effectiveness of the teaching pedagogy being implemented. Therefore, the regular use of assessments and feedback together with continuous reflection of the teacher on their strategies will be crucial to becoming good or excellent at teaching as this will enable one to ascertain if real learning is taking place or not. Obtaining student feedback on a more regular basis and not just at the end of the academic year will allow for changes to be made to the teaching approaches so that effective teaching is consistently achieved. Many HEIs give their students an opportunity to provide feedback on the quality of the module delivery by using what are known as Module Evaluation Questionnaires or MEQs for short which the students fill in usually at the end of every module studied in each academic year. What could be considered more useful would be to have the students fill out these questionnaires midway through their course of study as well as at the end to help the teacher better gauge the views of the class earlier and so any changes deemed necessary can be made more immediately by the teacher, hence improving the overall teaching and learning experience of students.

The importance of obtaining student feedback within the teaching session can be incredibly significant for both the student and the teacher in improving learning. To increase student engagement and to allow them to be able to discuss their understanding of the ideas presented, there must be ample opportunities for students to contribute to discussions related to the content being studied. This will allow for the teacher to determine if true understanding is taking place and crucially highlight any misconceptions the students may have, thus allowing for further guidance to be provided to the students to enable them to revaluate their understanding of the subject matter being taught.

Clearly, most academics will agree that delivering excellent teaching requires consistent dedication to ensure that sessions have been well-planned so that lectures are based more on the use of 'student-centred' rather than the traditional 'teacher-centred' approaches so that students are therefore more active and therefore more motivated to learn in depth about the subject matter in and outside of the classroom.

One of the most important considerations for some academics is the perceived incentives in teaching compared to the potential rewards that can arise from a high-profile research career which may involve numerous research publications and large grant captures that underpin career and promotion prospects as an academic. To address some of these concerns, there are now more opportunities available in many universities around the world for clearly defined career promotion routes for teaching and learning than was previously the case, enabling progression to professorial status based on teaching excellence with a status alongside that of the more traditional research professor.

Classification of Teaching Levels in HE

If academics are hoping for career promotion through advancement in teaching and learning, then there must be some clearly defined structure that determines and distinguishes how one is engaging with teaching and so ultimately is able to demonstrate the higher level of achievements in this area.

Kreber (2002) discusses three different ways in which academics can engage with teaching and these are classified as teaching excellence, teaching expertise and the highest level being the scholarship of teaching which are all considered in further detail below. Having a more clearly defined understanding of the quality levels of teaching taking place in HEIs will not only enable these institutions to monitor that minimum standards of teaching are being met but crucially will have well-defined career plans to promotion with incentives for continuous improvements in teaching standards. Academics will be able to concentrate and spend more time and effort in improving their teaching and learning while feeling secure in the knowledge that this has the potential for career development and promotion, whereas previously, they may have considered this time as being lost in comparison to time spent on generating research output and grant capture activities which were previously the only recognised avenues available for career promotions.

When analysing the academic literature in this subject area it becomes clear that there is no consensus of what is meant by the different categories of teaching excellence, teaching expertise or the scholarship of teaching. The Advance HE goal is to help shape the future of HEIs so that they enhance performance and strive for excellence in teaching and learning by encouraging academics to engage with the UKPSF. This excellence in teaching can develop because of one's own personal teaching experience and can be enhanced by reflective practice. This is a process of learning from experience by reflecting on one's own teaching practice and the results or outputs of the session and determining what could be done differently to improve the session. This is an essential process for achieving excellence in teaching. Work done by many educational theorists has indicated the importance of this 'reflective' practice in the overall learning process. Schön (1983) argued that this knowledge of teaching experience gained by teachers is acquired through 'reflection on action' and 'reflection in action'. This latter is essentially one thinking on one's feet and the former leads to building on previous experiences and thereby having different strategies to deal with a possible range of circumstances encountered in practice. Kolb (1984) proposes a multistage model called the experiential learning cycle which allows individuals to understand their experiences which then enables them to modify their behaviour accordingly through repeatedly reflecting on what they are doing.

When moving from the practitioner's personal experience in achieving teaching excellence to what constitutes teaching expertise, we need to consider how and to what extent educational theory can enhance teaching practice. Norris (2000) contends that practitioners need to be clear and understand that educational theories are only taken as 'models' that can be adapted as situations dictate them to be necessary rather than all-encompassing problem-solving teaching strategies. So, knowledge of learning theories will help teachers to understand better how people learn as well as why certain methods promote effective learning compared to others. To become a teaching expert requires continuous reflection on practice and how the learning experience of the students can be improved, thereby developing their own skill levels. In this way, teachers are then able to develop a greater number of problem-solving strategies and teaching expertise. In summary, when a teaching professional combines an in-depth subject knowledge with the knowledge of how best to teach in practice which is derived from both educational theories and from practical experience then one can be thought of as having teaching expertise.

Therefore, the question that arises is, what constitutes scholarship of teaching and how does this differ from teaching expertise? There is no one agreed definition for what is considered as the scholarship of teaching, but teaching scholars are considered both excellent teachers and expert teachers and that they go much further in sharing their knowledge to advance the knowledge of teaching and learning with their own colleagues as well as the wider teaching community. This sharing of practice takes different forms including: Journal Publications and Conference Presentations as well as in-house workshop activities within their own institutions. Fanghanel et al. (2016) discuss the role of scholarship of teaching and teaching in HE and they arrive at a general agreement in regarding what its key features are. Scholarship of teaching not only encompasses the analysis of teaching practice through critical reflection on what works well and what does not, as well as using education theories to enhance teaching practices but crucially, one must be able to disseminate the outcomes from findings for peer review and public scrutiny to further develop the teaching and learning processes. It is unlikely that most academics will achieve this level of scholarship of teaching as this may not be of interest to them, but for those whose passion it is to promote and improve teaching and learning it could bring with it potential rewards.

Incentives and Rewards in Teaching

What becomes evident from the above discussion is that the scholarship of teaching will be for the most enthusiastic academics who have decided to focus on teaching and learning in their academic careers. However, what is more noticeable across the HE sector is that some elements are being incorporated into staff appraisals and other key teaching and learning activities. With the current incentives at universities still being more focused on 'research' activities both internal and external, one may ask why academics would strive to become expert or scholars of teaching. Clearly, if there were similar incentives and rewards available to academics regarding teaching activities which were comparable with research activities then this would help to promote these goals.

Otherwise, there is a heavy reliance on intrinsic motivations which results in only a few highly motivated individuals engaging within this area of work in our HEIs.

HEIs that are genuinely trying to improve the teaching and learning experience of their students are relying on their teaching staff to achieve this. When designing schemes that are going to motivate staff to achieve this behaviour, clearly there must be incentives that are considered worthwhile. It is likely that for some staff if they can see potential rewards, then they are more likely to put greater effort into achieving this, rather than if the rewards are considered relatively insignificant.

However, it has been noted that one of the biggest challenges in designing effective incentive schemes is the ability to accurately determine and measure the desired behaviour intended of teaching staff, whether these are quantitative in nature such as exam marks or qualitative in nature such as from in-class teacher evaluations. So, considerations on schemes such as rewarding staff with pay bonuses that are based on these kinds of outcomes may seem attractive, but one quickly realises that in practice this becomes exceedingly difficult and complex to measure these outcomes with any certainty and reliability. One must always be careful of what can potentially develop with these situations: the tendency for some staff to start manipulating the system and getting involved in less than desirable activities. There is a danger with what was originally meant to increase a desired outcome, resulting instead in undesirable behaviour among staff pursuing these extra incentives.

However, what could be considered more practical to implement as an incentive is that all teaching staff could be required to achieve a minimum standard regarding their teaching and learning experience level through having to satisfactorily complete requirements for the 'Fellow' of the Advance HE before they are considered for moving from Lecturer to Senior Lecturer positions. Subsequently, for those looking for higher academic positions such as Principal Lecturer or Reader, a minimum requirement of 'Senior Fellow' of the Advance HE could be made as mandatory and finally with 'Principal Fellow' a prerequisite for those aiming to become Professors in teaching and learning. If HEIs begin implementing these requirements rigorously for all teaching staff and staff could therefore now clearly see potential pathways for career progression, then teaching and learning levels could also improve.

To help ensure that teaching and learning standards are raised in our HEIs, clearly defined incentives regarding progression and promotion in teaching and learning need to exist and be in place. For academics to strive to achieve and become expert teachers or scholars of teaching then clearly defined pathways to becoming Readers and Professors in teaching and learning must be available to them as is currently the case with research activities which attract grant captures.

E-learning and the Use of Technology

It is now the case that with the rapid advancements in technology all aspects of people's lives have been impacted by technology: this includes education and digital learning.

E-learning is learning conducted through computers and the internet using electronic media and is also known as online learning or sometimes online education.

Currently, it is still true that the traditional learning methods of classrooms filled with students being taught by subject expert academics form the main basis of the teaching and learning methodologies being implemented in most of the HEIs around the world (MacDonald et al., 2005). However, with so much information available to students via the internet, academics are no longer the only source of information they can turn to and so students have become more active in their own learning process and this is a positive outcome of the use of technology, but one must be aware that this can also lead to students being less focused and distracted more easily than ever before.

Clearly, the restrictions and limitations that exist with the traditional modes of face-to-face learning at universities of location and time are no longer of issue when one considers e-learning as with this mode of learning there is a great degree of flexibility and accessibility.

Historically, in the United Kingdom, the Open University was the first to promote widening access to education through their distance learning approach. Students were sent their course material through the post and studied for the most part on their own with the assistance of some televised programmes through the BBC usually scheduled late at night and some scheduled face-to-face learning sessions. Students would communicate with their course tutors through standard post which took time. With the advent of home computers and the internet this has now allowed for much faster communications between student and tutor as well as the Open University now being able to offer a much wider range of interactive educational experiences to their online students (Ellis et al., 2009).

These days most educational institutions at all the different levels up to and including HEIs have embraced the use of technology and now have some forms of Virtual Learning Environments (VLEs) for staff and student interaction. These VLEs have many integrated web-based applications that provide academics and students with information and useful resources that help support and enhance the educational experience of the students. Therefore, learning is clearly not just restricted to the classroom anymore and students are now able to continue to learn wherever they are located. Discussion on projects or group work can continue through group chat forums and submission of work can now be carried out online. Classes can now be conducted online at different institutions in multiple locations at the same time if required using software technology such as Microsoft Teams and Zoom. Both are a chat-based collaboration platform which are particularly suited to having online class sessions or meetings as required. Communication with one another is enabled through this software as it allows for online sessions to take place with many team members and in any location around the world as long as there is internet access available.

This mode enables specialist tuition to be easily included in the module through audiovisual materials or contributions directly from a specialist. Prior to VLE and digital learning the module tutor would have to make all the physical arrangements for the specialist visitor as well as acquiring permission and agreement to cover all their travel and accommodation costs. With the use of new technology and e-learning, most arrangements and associated costs no longer exist, and the specialist lecture can be delivered virtually using computer technology at both locations so that the students' experience is remarkably to that if the visitor was physically present in their classroom. What this technology now enables academics to do is to potentially access specialist resources from all over the world and so their students can utilise and benefit from the latest knowledge and information available in their subject areas as never before.

Given the advancements in technology, one must understand that people learn in different ways, and the use of e-learning tools such as chat rooms, message boards, instant messaging and even online classes is not necessarily a replacement for the more traditional communal learning. The traditional face-to-face approach has always been highly effective in that it has the capacity to generate thought-provoking discussions in the classroom between students. However, interactive technology can be an additional effective tool in enhancing the traditional form of learning. It may be the case that for those students who lack self-confidence and are therefore reluctant to talk in the classroom situation with others present, they are now more likely to contribute to discussions through these online channels of communications.

There is also the reality of technology having limitations in that specific programmes, for example, which require laboratory work and/or studio time or require hands-on experience of equipment, will not readily be suitable to online learning. Even though information and videos may be available on the subject matter to share and learn from, there will be no real substitution for allowing students to exercise the practical experience. However, even this concern may be put aside eventually, as ever-increasing advancements in interactive technology have enabled in some fields the use of realistic virtual reality applications and simulations such as that currently being used in the areas of medicine and in many engineering disciplines.

Conclusions

The concept of the scholarship of teaching may only be appealing to a small number of academics in disciplines other than those in education as educators are clearly involved in different kinds of scholarly activities. Excellence, expertise and scholarship of teaching are assuredly different in nature and so should be recognised accordingly.

One must marvel at how technology and particularly e-learning education has become so important and integral to educational institutions all over the world after the general universal shutdown and lockdown of countries that occurred around March 2020 due to the Covid-19 pandemic. It has to be pointed out that in the United Kingdom, with campus closures happening close to the end of the academic year, students only had a few weeks of classes left to attend and as such the number of online classes that needed to be covered was small. Had this closure happened much earlier in the academic year then the effectiveness of this en masse e-learning education for students may have been somewhat different and HEIs could have been facing more serious consequences with the possibility of students demanding the return of fees for lack of the traditional education they had originally signed up for. What e-learning has enabled is that education can continue to be given to students albeit in this distance learning format with online classes through using software such as 'Microsoft Teams' and recorded videos made available on 'Blackboard' as well as through many other electronic communication media. Even final examinations with some modification can still be carried out online in timed set periods for students to complete, ensuring that students can progress as well as graduate on time and therefore ensuring their careers are not detrimentally affected in anyway. Used appropriately and when necessary, technology can help to augment what is already in existence.

Chapter 4

METHODOLOGIES FOR IMPROVING TEACHING EXCELLENCE

It should be universally understood that there is a moral obligation on all Higher Education Institutions (HEIs) to provide their students with the highest quality of teaching standards possible. In countries where students must pay for their own Higher Education (HE), students are investing significant amounts of their own time and money in their HE studies and therefore they are customers expecting the highest quality academic experience in return. Before 1998, in the United Kingdom, HE was free for all students continuing to study for their first degree at the undergraduate level. A radical political shift in educational ethos in 1998 introduced student fees and loans. With this substantial level of personal investment, surely students must be entitled to value for money when it comes to the teaching quality they receive throughout the duration of their studies. This resulted in the introduction of the teaching quality assessment process across the HE sector: the Teaching Excellence Framework (TEF). This move to the marketisation of HE is not just a UK phenomenon but can be seen across many countries around the world and has resulted in the production of league tables for research and teaching along with 'student satisfaction' rates; these metrics are having a greater impact when it comes to institutions competing for student numbers. Clearly, now there is a greater emphasis than ever before on the teaching quality of universities, and it is vitally important to be able to measure accurately teaching excellence within the HE sector.

A contentious issue within HEIs is the notion of what constitutes 'teaching excellence' and more importantly if it can be measured. HE by its very nature provides a diversity of learning opportunities to students depending on the various disciplines studied from courses that are highly vocational in nature to the more theoretically based subjects. If teaching quality is to be measured, it could be more appropriately achieved through qualitative rather than quantitative measures. It may be possible to capture the main features, describe them and then use a guide to make judgements of what teaching excellence represents. From empirical studies carried out within HE, it is considered that an excellent teacher should be one that has the following attributes (Wood and Su, 2017; Kreber, 2002):

- Excellent knowledge of the subject matter
- Able to convey concepts easily
- Ability to motivate their students to learn
- Able to help students overcome difficulties in their learning
- Skilled in pedagogical approaches that encourage critical thinking and therefore independent learning
- Dedication and a committed professional

The academic's role in HE is complex in nature and is generally split between their teaching duties, research and related scholarly activities, their various organisational and administrative tasks together with the necessity for continuous professional development activities which are required for professional body requirements on certain courses. How much time one spends on these different requirements depends generally on the academic's specialism as either a continually active researcher or primarily a teaching practitioner. Academic staff appointed at universities generally are expected to have higher degrees and have also been trained and tested in research and have some peer-reviewed publications attributed to them to prove their research competence. Today, academics are also expected to have some training in relation to teaching and learning through certified courses; however, it is generally more difficult to get objective evidence on their effectiveness as teachers as this is more difficult to assess. Also, it is an accepted norm within the HE sector that teaching excellence can be found when the teacher is actively engaging in teaching practices both through accepted pedagogical theories and practical implementations as well as enabling the active engagement of their students in the learning process.

Clearly, from our previously defined criteria of what constitutes excellent teaching, there is a convergence of a combination of different attributes including specialist knowledge, thorough lesson and activity planning, a range of useful strategies, a focus on a more student-centred approach and continuous reflection on one's practice. The remainder of this chapter considers some of the different approaches that could be considered as ways in which teaching excellence can be enhanced in the classroom and thereby improve the overall learning experience of students. These different approaches or methodologies tend to encompass one or more of the above-mentioned criteria, thus promoting and facilitating teaching excellence. The approaches presented here are by no means exhaustive and are just some examples of the ways in which teaching quality could be enhanced.

Use of Educational Theory and Self-Regulated Learning

In the United Kingdom and in many other countries around the world, academics working in HEIs are expected now to have some form of teaching qualification such as a PGCE certificate or some other form of teaching and learning recognition. As a 'Fellow' of the Advance HE, academics with substantive teaching and supporting learning roles should have sufficient knowledge of and be able to show a general understanding of effective approaches to learning and teaching.

It is generally accepted among academics that to a large degree, their knowledge about what is effective teaching derives from reflecting on their personal teaching experience (Schön, 1983). What happens in practice is that teaching methods that tend to work well are kept and those that are found to be not so good or did not work well are discarded. In this way through 'reflection' and over time the academic builds a range of approaches or strategies that are felt to work well and are effective and so are therefore used on a regular basis. So, can this approach to teaching be improved further? Norris (2000) suggests that this personal knowledge gained by the academic through their practical experience can be further enhanced if combined with the theoretical knowledge from educational research. The general theories of Teaching and Learning which represent 'general models' of how people learn fall into categories such as Behaviourism, Constructivism, Experiential Learning, Pedagogy and Andragogy (Gravells and Simpson, 2014). Although a detailed description of all the different learning theories is not present here, it can be said that a significant shift in educational thinking has occurred in the last 30 to 40 years to acknowledge a move away from the view that learning is a passive activity where teachers deliver from the front and students who are motivated will naturally be learning by listening attentively. Along with the teacher's positive and negative reinforcements, the desired outcomes of learning could be achieved. Teachers acting in a particular way will mean that students likewise act in a certain desired way, leading to the theory that is known as 'behaviourism'. Subsequently, a new approach to learning emerged, one in which the learners' 'mind' plays an important role in the learning process. Learners can acquire knowledge and try to make sense of the world around them through engaging in various tasks such as reading, socialising, interacting with the environment and taking personal responsibility for being their own active learners. This kind of learning is generally considered as the 'constructivist' approach to learning and replaced the earlier behaviourist approach to learning.

So, if the models of teaching and learning are understood and can be adapted by the academic's particular needs to see what fits most appropriately within their teaching context, then they can compile valid forms of information about teaching alongside their practical knowledge base gained through practical experience. It can then be argued that to be a more effective teacher, one must reflect on both the personal teaching experience and on the extent to which educational research theories can explain those approaches.

To become even more effective as a teacher one cannot remain static with regard to the teaching strategies being used. Academics cannot rely exclusively on the same strategies that were developed by reflection through practical experience early in their careers and then just rigidly stick to them throughout the rest of their careers. Surely to continue to improve, one must continually engage in reflective thinking about their approaches and ask which worked and which did not and most importantly why they worked or did not work. Addressing specific problems encountered in their practice and finding potential solutions to solve them can make academics more effective than they were previously. With this self-monitoring and self-evaluation process taking place alongside the reflective process, the whole process becomes one of self-regulated learning and the individuals who actively engage in this process develop into even more effective teachers than those that do not. It is this desire of self-regulation to continue to seek to be even more effective as a teacher that will ultimately help raise the teaching quality standards in academia.

Student-Centred Learning Approaches

There are two main concepts of teaching that can be classified as either teacher-centred and content-oriented versus the student-centred and learning-oriented approaches to teaching and learning (Kember, 1997). A problem with student-centred learning is that it can mean a range of different meanings to people across the educational spectrum. In the teacher-centred approaches, the teacher is a transmitter of knowledge to the student who receives the knowledge, that is, from the expert to the novice, whereas in the student-centred approach, the emphasis is on the students' learning and what they do to achieve this learning rather than what the teacher does (Harden and Crosby, 2000). In the latter the importance is given to what the student is doing. Student-centred learning is based on the constructivist theories of education. Rather than the traditional approach of rote learning, students *construct* knowledge and meaning through new experiences and interactions (Carlile and Jordan, 2005). Table 4 compares the main features of these two approaches to learning and what the student's role is in each category.

Table 4 Student-centred versus teacher-centred learning

Student-Centred Learning	Teacher-Centred Learning
Teacher as a facilitator	Teacher as the expert
Learning activities/spaces are flexible	Rigid rows of desks
Students active and doing	Students are passive
Students have choices	There is little student choice
Student led	Teacher led
Formative assessments	Testing and grade focused

In the context of teaching across the spectrum of a whole range of different subject areas in HE, one cannot say that learning can be distinctly represented as either wholly student centred or teacher centred. There is generally a continuum between the student-centred and teacher-centred learning where it may be more appropriate to be operating at an optimum along this continuum to achieve the best results for any subject being taught. What can be said is that the solely teacher-focused transmission of information approaches to teaching such as the standard lecture or the reading from a PowerPoint presentation where students are just the passive recipients of information are not considered as the most effective ways to enhance student learning. What is apparent is that the student-centred learning approaches are intrinsically linked to the constructivist view of learning which rely on the students as active participants engaged in related and associated learning activities. If the teacher thinks about one of the most important questions of how one knows if learning is taking place in the classroom, then surely activities need to be in place to be able to measure students' learning. The more student activities that can be introduced into the classroom such as individual problem-solving, discussions with colleagues, group work activities, quizzes and even an introduction of a few minutes where students can provide feedback on key concepts that they continue to struggle with can all help to facilitate the enhancement of the learning process. To be truly student-centred, the student must be able to direct what they are wanting to learn and in which ways they can learn as well. Students must also be able to track how they are progressing and have clarity about what is the success criteria for them. Using a process of formative assessment then allows the student to understand how they are progressing and therefore allow them to determine what needs to be done to make further improvements. Clearly, there are subjects that can make use of a wholly student-centred approach to learning and then there will be other subjects that will require a significant teacher contribution in terms of information and knowledge at the beginning of the class, and finding the right balance is the key to maximising the learning experience of the students for any subject being taught.

Within the context of the subject matter being taught, it is important to consider what is necessary in terms of approaches, for example, using either or both the teacher-centred to the student-centred learning approach or perhaps a combination. Some of the areas for consideration for practical implementation of a more student-centred approach are the areas of curriculum design, the modes of assessment used and the different teaching and learning methodologies that can be employed to facilitate this process.

In relation to curriculum design, to move to a student-centred learning approach one can consider what the learner can actively do rather than the teacher solely being expected to cover the entire content. Therefore, having learning outcomes that indicate explicitly what the student should be able to do rather than just what content needs to be covered pushes the emphasis more towards being able to accurately measure student competencies. Students having a greater choice in what they can study is also an important element in this process; however, this may be easier in some subject disciplines compared to others. Courses that are accredited by professional bodies may find it somewhat challenging to have a variety of different options made available to students in comparison to other subject areas. Incorporating active learning in the classroom with problem-solving activities can help to promote and facilitate students taking part and doing things for themselves and can allow for mechanisms that determine if real learning is taking place or not.

Some discipline areas such as Medicine and Dentistry have moved more towards a curriculum design that can be considered as wholly student-centred, known as Problem-Based Learning or PBL for short. Here, students assisted by a facilitator set their own learning outcomes through real-world scenarios that encourages them to develop a fuller understanding of the subject matter (O'Neill and McMahon, 2005). Again, with any new system that is implemented, it can take some time to evaluate its results and outcomes and with the PBL approach, many universities across the United Kingdom have made some modifications to their Medicine curriculum and now also include the more traditional lecture-based teaching alongside PBL to produce a hybrid curriculum design that attempts to include the best of the different approaches to teaching and learning.

Assessments are generally categorised as being either summative or formative. Summative assessments such as final written closed book examinations for awarding marks and grades and to make judgements on performance are used extensively throughout most HEIs. More formative assessments which give students valuable feedback on their learning and help identify essential gaps in knowledge and understanding can be of greater benefit to the student, thereby enhancing the student learning process. The ability of the student to self-assess is critical in the process to help the student to take more responsibility for their own learning and so is an important element in the student-centred learning approach. A range of formative assessments can be employed from giving verbal and written feedback on assignment and essays to making use of short quizzes that assess knowledge and understanding. These formative assessments can help identify the strengths, weaknesses and key areas for further development.

Looking at the different teaching and learning methodologies that can be employed that promote student-centred learning, one must be careful to realise that what works well for one subject area may not be as effective in others. What is important is that the key components that make for a student-centred approach are that the students are active in acquiring the skill and knowledge base as well as the student being aware of why they are doing the activities and how these are related to 'real-world' applications. Approaches of teaching and learning that encourage small or large group work, discussions and opportunities for all students to participate in tasks, students being able to present their work and even a very small time allocated for writing reflections on their learning towards the end of the class sessions are just some of the ways that promote a more student-centred approach to learning in the classroom.

There is evidence-based research that shows that student-centred learning is an effective approach to teaching and learning, but one must also be aware that it may not be an easy method to employ in many places where there are extremely limited resources with different cultures and attitudes to learning. For those practitioners who currently operate a more teacher-centred approach, some of the changes proposed here may be too much of a change to be employed at once and so consideration could be given to making some smaller incremental changes that help in moving the continuum towards a more student-centred learning approach.

The 'Flipped' Classroom

This approach to learning moves away from the traditional model of learning which is based on the teacher-centred model where teachers are the transmitters of information and the students are the passive learners, having assigned work to complete usually in their own time at home. With the advancement of digital technology, a new learning approach known as the 'flipped' classroom has emerged initially from work carried out in United States in the mid-2000s. With a traditional lecturing approach, the teacher will deliver new material content at the beginning of the classroom and then students will be expected

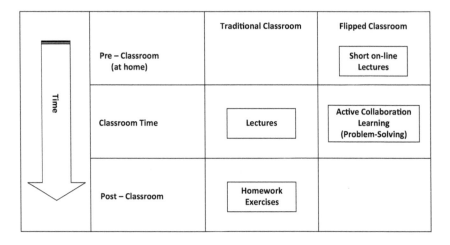

Figure 4 The differences in the traditional classroom model and the Flipped class-room model.

to understand the material and tackle associated problems in-class, possibly leaving the more challenging problems to do on their own usually at home. In the 'flipped' classroom model the situation is reversed with the teachers posting short video lectures online for students to view in their own time at home before attending the lecture or making available literature to be studied before attending the class. Class time is then spent on expanding and mastering the material through discussion and collaborative learning exercises. Here the teacher acts more as a facilitator and students are able to help each other in the learning process, that is, peer-to-peer learning. This type of pedagogy has now been rated as one of the top trends in educational technology. The 'flipping' here refers to the more challenging homework being carried out in class time, and the lectures which are usually done in class time are viewed at home by the students. Studies carried out at Nottingham Trent University in the United Kingdom show from data that using this 'flipped' model approach to learning across a large proportion of their taught modules, students from minority groups tended to perform better in these type of models compared to the more traditional models (The Guardian, 2019). The best way of showing how this model works and compares with the traditional models of teaching is through a schematic diagram shown in Figure 4.

The main objective of the 'flipped' classroom approach is to improve student learning by reversing the traditional model of a classroom and by focusing the class time on students' understanding of the subject matter by actively engaging in activities compared to listening to standard lectures.

Table 5 The advantages and disadvantages of using the 'Flipped' classroom model

Flipped Classroom Model

Advantages	Disadvantages
Students having more control:	*Students must be prepared in advance:*
Students have more freedom to view the short lectures at their own pace at home and as many times as required for better understanding of the material. Better prepared to ask questions in the classroom.	Since the students are expected to have watched the lectures at home prior to attending class, it relies on trusting the students to participate fully and there is no guarantee this can be achieved.
Encourages student-centred learning and collaboration:	*Labour intensive for the teacher:*
Class time is now utilised through discussions and group work with students able to help each other and so students are more active in learning rather than passive recipients.	The making of the smaller home lecture videos requires time and expertise. The appropriate student-centred activities used in class to motivate the students to prepare well all require additional time and effort.
Lectures and content are more accessible: With the lectures available as online videos, these can be always accessed. Also, students who have had to miss classes due to valid reasons can also catch up more quickly.	*All students need to have access to technology:* To view the home lectures, students need to have access to a computer and have the internet. This may be more difficult for students from poorer income families compared to others.

As with all pedagogical models there are advantages and disadvantages with implementation and how effective they are.

Some of the main advantages and disadvantages of this model are outlined in Table 5.

To make the 'flipped' classroom approach successful, there must be a commitment by both the students and the teachers. Clearly, this approach relies on and is dependent on students having engaged with the set material before attending the class and there can be no assurances that all students will cooperate with this. Also, there is a genuine concern that teachers will see this model requiring a lot of extra work in preparation beforehand compared to the more traditional approaches of teacher-centred learning, and so this additional preparation must be accounted for in the workload model of academics ensuring that adequate time has been given to make this approach work effectively.

Overall, the 'flipped classroom' method to learning seems to be gaining in popularity at all levels within the educational system from high school through to university level, with students having a much more hands-on approach to learning.

Technology-Enabled Learning

When one considers incorporating technology into the classroom, what immediately comes to mind is the use of digital technology to enhance learning. The technology of the past largely consisted of the use of chalkboard, textbooks and information displayed on the walls of the classroom. Now, in the digital age, there is an increasing need for the teacher to have a greater understanding of how to integrate new digital technological resources into course content and pedagogy. There is an abundant amount of digital technological resources available in most HEIs that began with the introduction of electronic whiteboards or 'smartboards' in every classroom to the now ubiquitous Virtual Learning Environment (VLE). The additional developments of Skype, blogs, wikis, MP3 players, iPads, podcasts, e-textbooks, smartphones and virtual reality show that the technologies just appear to keep evolving each year. The use of this technology in the classroom must be to *enhance* the students' learning experience and not for using technology for its own sake just because it happens to be there. One of the biggest hurdles to overcome in the use of these appropriate technologies is that academics must first become familiar and comfortable with the different applications that accompany these new technologies. This will generally require staff training, development and education to make sure that staff are able to embed these technologies appropriately into their course content to enhance the learning experience of the student. These staff development programmes must address the needs of academics and therefore should ideally have their input in the design process of the workshops needed and there also needs to be opportunity for plenty of interaction and reflection to take place.

Once the full potential use of these technologies has been realised then academics are able to use their pedagogies of learning combined with the use of technologies to enhance their own teaching practices. As an example of the potential benefits of the VLE rather than just only being used as a repository for storing course documentation and course content, it can be developed further to benefit students even outside of the normal classroom. If beneficial, many activities such as quizzes, wikis and forums can be set online where students can interact with the teacher and with each other and so enabling learning to continue beyond the normal boundaries of the traditional classroom environment. There are many other areas within education where new technologies that are being used are having profound effects on the students' learning experience. The use of virtual reality simulators in supporting students' learning in the subject area of human anatomy within medicine is a good example of how students can get valuable experiences of working with cadavers before working on the real corpse in the laboratories. This new technological application can add virtual value to the students' learning experience because the interactions between muscles, organs, nerves and blood vessels can be seen that was not previously possible with actual dissections of cadavers.

HEIs are increasingly making use of new technological applications to enhance the learning experience of students which is evident in 'blended learning' that is now taking place using VLEs. It is envisaged that academics will be able to maximise the student learning experience with technological applications as a valuable tool to aiding them, thereby raising the overall teaching quality standards.

Academics entering HEIs generally begin as a subject specialist in their chosen subject areas such as Engineering, Law or Medicine, for example. Professionals are then expected to continue additional training in pedagogy via various teacher training courses. To improve and achieve excellence in teaching, an understanding and interaction of these two knowledge bases must be achieved and put into practice. However, with new technologies increasing and being readily available, there is now an even greater need to combine these new developments with known and successful pedagogical methods such as active learning, for example. This technological knowledge should not just be restricted to having an awareness but also how it can be applied practically and implemented most appropriately in the classroom as well as in the VLEs. It is envisaged that as academics become more familiar and comfortable with the available technology for their subject areas, their use of technology will increase, but what always must be paramount to them is that effective pedagogy is the driving force and central to effective teaching and learning. Clearly, academics who decide to make use of the latest technology should not just use technology for technology's sake but as an integral learning tool. What must always be remembered is not to lose sight of the true purpose of using the technology which is to facilitate and enhance the learning process of the students.

Gamification Techniques

The ever-increasing presence of new technology in the learning environment has resulted in a move from traditional classroom lectures to increased integrated digital learning environments. The introduction and incorporation of game elements in pedagogy is another way that can help to evolve the teaching process to promote greater competition among students, create effective teamwork and enhance student communication skills.

It is well understood that an effective way of learning especially for young children is through play which can help develop skills such as inquiry and teamwork. Indeed, many renowned education theorists including Vygotsky have argued that play is a crucial component of the cognitive development process in humans throughout their different development stages (Veresov, 2016).

How students engage with teaching and learning activities within the learning environment has an important bearing on their ultimate achievement and performance (Handelsman et al., 2005). Finding ways to keep students engaged within lessons is a constant challenge faced by educators, and studies have shown that active students are more likely to perform well as they tend to retain more knowledge during their learning activities (Mohd et al., 2016).

Gamification is the use of game design elements in non-game settings to engage participants and encourage desired behaviours. Research studies have referred to gamification as a technique that can be used to increase student engagement within the learning environment (Hanus and Fox, 2015). While gamification relates to gaming, it is not about turning an activity into playing nor is it about developing games for learning. Rather, gamification is about using game elements in non-game activities such as learning to create a game-like experience in such activities. Thus, gamification can be considered as another student-centred approach to learning in which the students are active participants in the classroom and not just passive recipients of information. In HE some of the main important game elements that can be incorporated to motivate and encourage student learning are challenges, narratives, progression, feedback and elements of choice.

There may be barriers that need addressing before most academics can adopt gamification strategies into their lesson plans, not least a reluctance for many to move away from the more familiar traditional lecture-based delivery mode and the lack of support and training made available to academics to incorporate these advance technologies into their classrooms. However, fortunately there are now many game-based online learning platforms that allow for the easy creation, sharing and playing of games or trivia quizzes very quickly. Kahoot is a typical example of this software that easily allows for designing short quizzes which can be delivered at the start of each class, testing how much understanding of the previous study has taken place and allowing for formative feedback between teachers and students. This can be a fun and competitive way to engage the students in the material to be learned as the students can easily use their mobile devices to log in and participate real-time in the activity. There are other many free software tool platforms such as Quizlet and Socrative that allow for similar developments of quiz games.

In relation to STEM-based subject areas where mathematical symbols and equations are needed, a software tool like Microsoft Forms has a quiz option that allows the design of easy and quick formative or summative assessments using incorporated mathematical functions' options that make designing assessment quizzes much easier than ever before. In education, feedback is important in any learning process and may fulfil different roles such as to provide encouragement, advice and general confirmation in the learning process.

In other subjects where students require good discussion and debating skills, a conversation game like 'Mixed Company' allows students to have meaningful conversations around current topics that they are learning about while applying real-world context and ideas to concepts they are studying. This is another excellent game which embedded into the session can encourage students to learn effectively and develop good discussion and debating skills.

The use of points and badges as game elements is commonly used in non-game settings as well as in education (Dicheva et al., 2014). It is the case that in many learning situations the student performance in assignments and tests is calculated in terms of marks or points achieved. In these circumstances, points are considered ways to communicate progress and attainment as well as acknowledging the students' efforts made. Making use of progressive learning skills can be incorporated readily into curriculum design where students are given a test to complete at the end of a topic and only by achieving a certain minimum level of success can they progress to the next topic; otherwise they must return and revise previous material to successfully complete the test. The potential benefits of this progressive learning process for the student are that by being successful in the former parts of the course they will have hopefully gained the necessary skills to be able to successfully complete the latter parts.

The choice element of gaming can also be easily applied to an educational setting by allowing students a say in the way their classes are structured. If students can have some input into the content of the class, then they are more likely to engage with the activities available. An example could be by having multiple assignment choices available with different point weightings attached to them and the students can choose different assignment combinations if their total points meet a set target. Since students have a range of diverse preferred learning styles, this notion of different options opens up various ways to learning, some choosing to write an essay compared to a group discussion task while still achieving the overall desired learning outcomes for the module.

In summary, gamification can be viewed as an additional tool available to educators to add to their existing teaching and learning approaches. It can be used to gamify certain learning activities to make teaching effective by encouraging students to actively engage with the different learning activities.

Relating Theory and Practice

When considering the best ways of incorporating technologies into the classroom one must always have in mind in what ways these are going to advance the teaching and learning experience in the classroom. Asking important questions such as 'How does technology fit into my teaching?' and looking deeply into ways of incorporating technology into the curriculum are important considerations for all academics today and especially in the future as the range of technological applications available increases.

In the design of curriculum for effective teaching and learning the student should ideally wherever possible be able to relate the theory being taught in the classroom to its use and implementation in the real world. Clearly, students will have a greater understanding of the material being studied once they can see how it is used and fits into the workplace. Consideration here is given to two methodologies that aim to give students greater understanding of theory and practice, the first is that of using simulation as a teaching approach and the other of giving students work-based learning (WBL) experience.

Simulation technology

Simulation generally refers to the imitation of real-world activities and processes within a safe environment. Simulation is a general and flexible teaching approach that can be used across many disciplines. It is particularly useful in areas where role-play can be achieved or where students need to develop skills and experience but where cost considerations, safety issues or time constraints prevent this happening in the real world.

A key component of simulation is that it is a dynamic experience for the student with active engagement helping learners explore their decision-making and outcomes with the added advantage of allowing learners the opportunity to try alternative approaches if needed. There are many well-established disciplines that make amazingly effective use of simulation such as the use of medical simulators that allow students to practice their diagnosis and treatment on 'mannequins' that can react back in a realistic manner. Clearly, in these situations it would be highly dangerous to allow medical students to practise on real patients and so simulation provides the next best opportunity for virtual learning. With advancements in virtual reality and mixed reality technology, medical students are now able to learn far more effectively and understanding is increased rather than just with traditional lectures and textbooks. In many engineering disciplines simulation plays a critical role from prototype design processes to flight simulators where students can experience aircraft dynamics while never having to leave the ground. In our own institution, large investment into simulation technology known as 'Hydro-Minerva' technology has meant that areas such as Policing and Fire Management are able to give their students valuable hands-on experience of command-and-control situations of potential hazards in the real world which would otherwise not be possible. There are ever-increasing subject areas such as Business Management where simulation can allow for decision-making to take place and potential consequences seen without any of the risks that could result in the real world such as bankruptcy ever happening. What can be seen is that simulation allows for discussion and effective learning to take place even if the outcomes are not as predicted.

Another important area of technology that is impacting on education is Artificial Intelligence (AI). AI usually refers to the simulation of human intelligence in machines (computer systems) that are programmable to think like humans and mimic their actions. So, what does AI look like in education? There are currently online learning platforms available that can start with a diagnostic assessment of the students' current knowledge base in a range of subjects. The system builds up a picture of the students' level of understanding from the responses made. When the student then wants to learn more about a topic, the system can analyse the results from the assessment and then adjust the topic areas to study to accommodate any knowledge gaps found in the student. Only when the student gives correct responses will progress to the next topic be possible while continuously the system updates their level of understanding. This then allows for differentiated individualised learning to take place in classrooms with large student numbers, which would not be possible for teachers to do working on their own. Where could all this be leading to in the future as AI becomes even more sophisticated? It may be possible soon for computer systems to recognise and read facial expressions that indicate when someone is struggling to understand the material they are studying and therefore be able to modify the curriculum to meet their needs better. There are many other potential benefits of AI technology that can assist the teacher to become even more effective in their roles (Marr, 2019).

Work-based learning

Students studying in HEIs for undergraduate or postgraduate degrees are ultimately looking to utilise these qualifications in securing relevant employment. WBL can be an excellent way to help students gain a better understanding of what work experience really entails and aiding students in making their long-term career decisions.

WBL is an educational strategy that enables students to gain hands-on real-life experience of the workplace where they can use the academic knowledge acquired to develop their employability, in essence, allowing students to learn how the things they learn in the classroom are connected to the real world.

Although gaining popularity within the HE sector, WBL has not yet been fully embraced in all universities within the United Kingdom (Abraham, 2012). There are different models of WBL that are currently employed within the HE sector. The student can make use of internships which are usually short-term work experience in an organisation which can be paid or unpaid and usually carried out during the student holiday period. There are also valuable worksite field trips that can be embedded within curriculum design which give a general guided tour of a business and allow an opportunity to learn about the work processes and skill requirements for the different job roles within the organisation. There are the more traditional 'sandwich' courses especially in the United Kingdom which are usually four-year degree programmes in which after two years of university study the student is in a 'sandwich' or industrial placement which may comprise of their third year spending time working in a related industry or studying abroad depending on the nature of degree. The student then returns to complete their degree qualification in Year 4. Again, this experience gives the students a greater understanding of the real world, allowing the student to put into practice the theory learnt in the classroom. This type of experience can sometimes be invaluable for the student when applying for jobs as someone who can demonstrate having relevant work experience compared to other applicants who may have just studied the usual traditional three-year degree programme.

In the United Kingdom there has been a push by the government for universities to develop their WBL provision. Since 2015, some degree and higher apprenticeships have been available. As part of their apprenticeship, students can gain a full bachelor's or master's degree by working and studying part-time together. The content of these programmes has been developed by employers, universities and professional bodies working in partnership, with the aim of giving students relevant work experience combined with the necessary underpinning theory required. These degree apprenticeships are a further development of the internships and sandwich degrees as discussed above. There are clear differences for the students studying on a degree apprenticeship in that they will have no tuition fees to pay back, and they are employed as salaried staff from the beginning of their programme. In addition, employers work closely with universities in the co-design and development of a new degree apprenticeship programme, enabling them to have a greater input in the overall apprentice training.

Conclusions

With an ever-increasing number of students entering HE, the number of students entering with non-traditional qualifications has also increased. Students entering through access courses and having lower entry point grades increases the diversity and range of academic ability of the cohort of students in the classroom and lecture theatres. Historically, most students entering university generally had a high level of academic ability (presenting with good A Level grades) and were expected to be mostly independent learners who could turn to textbooks for extra support if required. Today, times have changed and a significant number of contemporary students lack key underpinning skills at entry to the programme and are not necessarily able to understand and cope with the course content through independent learning. The traditional approach to teaching with standard lectures delivered at the front of the class and students as passive learners cannot address the teaching and learning needs of a great many students now entering HE. Academics must continuously be reflective practitioners who examine their teaching approaches and are able to evaluate what works well and what does not and so be able to make improvements to their teaching methodologies as required. A move from the student as a passive recipient of information to a more active participant in his or her own learning process using more student-centred learning methodologies is required. The methodologies presented here are just some ways in which academics can develop the teacher/student-centred continuum to enhance the teaching and learning process in the classroom and to hopefully enhance teaching excellence. Clearly, it is expected that for some academics who use predominantly teacher-centred learning approaches, even making some small changes could bring about significant improvements in the students' overall teaching and learning experience.

Chapter 5

CONCLUSIONS

The Importance of Teaching Excellence

Teaching Excellence remains both a high priority and an elusive measurement. It remains a high priority partly due to the commercialisation of Higher Education (HE) which reconfigures 'Teaching' as a product to be valued, commodified and sold, and it remains elusive to measure because teaching is always only one-half of the equation, paired as it is with 'learning'. Although 'Learning and Teaching' are often put together as if two sides of the same coin, educators and students alike will know that they do not always occupy the same space. Sometimes learning can occur totally independent of teaching, often through circumstance, reflection and experience. Likewise teaching, even good teaching, requires a fertile audience to result in impactful learning. The emphasis within the HE sector has placed 'Teaching' at the heart of the agenda, without fully acknowledging the role that learners play in their own education. This places the emphasis on the part of the process which is costed in financial terms and less on the social and personal investment required from learners if they are to succeed. The responsibility is placed upon the educator and the educational establishment to ensure that learning is taking place. This in no way negates the importance of teaching excellence or the role of the teacher, but it is interesting that a two-way process is often viewed through a single, institutionally based lens. Interestingly institutions are seeking to actively engage students more readily in learning and to provide them with insights on how to learn effectively as an adjunct on how to be successful. But this part of the equation is also quantified by the organisation's success in engaging students; the responsibility is perceived as essentially that of the university. This configuration of learners as passive within the learning process and the recipients of initiatives, knowledge, innovations and information is at times a problematic one in that it leads institutions to be involved in ever more complex arrangements to engage students. The language of HE is often about 'attracting' students to courses, programmes and institutions. Therefore the offer must be rendered 'attractive' – buildings, estates, timetables, value-added experience – and although all of these are important, there can be a tendency to overlook the need for students to be clear on what they want to learn and be ready and equipped to learn it. Perhaps one of the key issues to consider in relation to 'teaching excellence' is 'student readiness'. This is not just about prior qualifications and clarity of direction but about helping students to understand how they learn and being enabled to select learning patterns and resources which suit their needs.

The Covid-19 pandemic of 2020 put into sharp focus how quickly experiences can change. The HE sector responded rapidly and comprehensively to put information online and allow students to continue with their studies. With differing degrees of success and with varying resources in digital capability, most institutions were able to flip their provision to online learning. Staff and students demonstrated adaptability in relation to the agility with which they adopted new learning styles and new mechanisms for learning. Preferences as to how to learn and how to teach were overturned by the necessity of the continuation of teaching. This led to lots of discussion and debate internally within institutions as to what constitutes teaching excellence. It could be argued that one element of excellence was consistency, continued provision, maintained standards and clarity of purpose. It could also be argued that maintenance of a programme and learning provision does not constitute excellence if the experience of learning is significantly changed, potentially impacting the student experience negatively. Some disciplinary areas reported increased student engagement with higher levels of attendance and greater use of online resources. Some of this may have been the result of work and other social commitments of students being lessened during lockdown. But it could also be about an increased engagement arising from a new set of expectations and a new set of common practices. It is often easier (technology permitting) to attend online without the need to relocate geographically. It is easier to be able to revisit concepts with asynchronous learning and to deconstruct sessions. It may just be the case that a wholesale move to an alternative mode of learning illuminated how change makes people re-evaluate and takes learning back to basics. There have been Covid-19-related challenges for educators and tutors alike. Transferring provision quickly online is not the same as preparing pedagogically for e-learning and online teaching. The loss of social connection, studio time, lab work and other areas has been problematic for disciplines, but the shift towards re-evaluating whole programmes piece by piece to see if and how they will work remotely and making decisions about the key elements of learning has had a huge impact on learning and teaching practices. The argument is not that remote or online learning is better but rather that a forced change leads to re-evaluation of the practice of learning and teaching and casts light on new areas for consideration. The longing of some staff and students to return to the classroom has opened up the debate about what 'classrooms' intrinsically mean for people and how they contribute to learning.

Another consideration is that learning is not just the achievement of qualifications or awards, although this is how it is measured and evaluated. Learning is about change, either in practice or the understanding and rationale for practice; it is about applied knowledge which becomes integrated into the lived experience of the learner. This is as applicable to learning about teaching as it is to other subjects. The emphasis on teaching qualifications and recognition of teaching practice is helpful and constructive but at best remains an unreliable way of measuring what it is to teach well and how to be a good teacher. The strengths of a good teacher and the essence of good teaching often reside in the gaps between measurements. This is the elusive 'something' which enables an individual to explain the complex, to stand beside the student and understand how they learn and what hinders learning and the passionate interest in a subject area which can be so infectious. The pursuit of learning and teaching skills has recently been elevated by the development of courses, awards and recognition, and rightly so, to become more of a formulated and rewarded career trajectory for academic staff. But even those who welcome that recognition, for themselves and for the sector, recognise the difficulties in quantifying teaching in terms of criteria – the animated, creative, dynamic practice of teaching is hard to place within linear boundaries. The problem remains a persistent one, we know when we are recipients of good teaching, we may be self-aware enough to know when we are teaching well, but it is harder to capture and contain those elements in frameworks and systems.

Internal and External Drivers for Improvements

There are multiple external and internal drivers for teaching excellence. The Teaching Excellence Framework (TEF), Office for Students (OfS), League Tables and National Student Survey (NSS) are all key elements of an emphasis on teaching excellence. Stakeholders, professional statutory bodies and employers also have a role in driving teaching excellence, and parents, teachers and career advisors may also utilise metrics to guide student decision-making. Internally the drivers can be conceptualised as relating to staff and student experience.

One of the largest changes is the TEF which seeks to evaluate and quantify teaching and to compare teaching quality between disciplines and where appropriate across institutions. The TEF, correlating as it does to the Research Excellence Framework (REF) and Knowledge Exchange Framework (KEF), is a key measure within HE. The TEF requires institutions to identity and capture elements of teaching excellence and consistency across the organisation. The stated objective is for achievement of a higher ranking in the TEF to become a mechanism to enable Higher Education Institutions (HEIs) to charge a higher rate for student fees, therefore the TEF potentially has a financial as well as reputational imperative. The OfS actively supports teaching excellence and innovation; as the regulator for HE it has a role in ensuring that students are encouraged to be involved. League Tables are increasingly important to institutions in terms of perceptions about teaching provision, reputation and quality of programmes. League Tables focus attention on the identified measurable elements. The NSS seeks the views of learning and teaching from final year undergraduate students. It is not clear how much attention is paid to the NSS by potential students planning to apply for a programme of study, but the results may influence careers, advisors, teachers and others in the guidance they give to school leavers. These however are not the only influences on teaching excellence; increasingly through work-based learning programmes, degree apprenticeships and placement-based vocational degrees, employers and stakeholders have a direct impact not only on learning in the workplace but also on the quality of the preparation for placement. This aspect of teaching and learning is less easy to quantify as students on vocational programmes may not fully understand the responsibilities of the two organisations working together. Pressures in the workplace can result in an impact on their view of 'teaching' on the work-based learning element, without recognition that this process is separated from university-based learning in terms of delivery and evaluation. Professional Bodies, particularly in relation to vocationally based learning, also play a role in determining core curriculum, teaching and learning priorities and the emphasis on the learning experience. This may include regulations as to the number of work-based hours and proportion of the course taught in university.

The internal drivers in HE are often related to the external drivers, ensuring that excellence in teaching and learning is accurately reflected in the metrics in League Tables and NSS. This is accompanied by Learning and Teaching strategies which demonstrate the learning and teaching priorities of an institution and shape how teaching is organised and evaluated. This will include measures such as peer observation of teaching and learning, support for internal and external recognition of learning and teaching through teacher training programmes, accreditation and recognition and application for awards such as the National Teaching Fellowships (NTFs). The NTF scheme aims to recognise individuals who have made outstanding impact on student outcomes and the teaching profession in HE each year. Clearly, achieving an NTF award is a way in which academics can gain national and international recognition in teaching and learning and thereby enhancing the prospects for those seeking career progression in this area. Increasingly the promotional structure for academics focused on teaching and learning also highlights teaching excellence in progression to teaching Fellow status, Readerships and Professorial positions in learning and teaching.

Role of Staff Development and Educational Programmes

Staff development plays an important role in teaching excellence. This stretches from the emphasis on learning and teaching in induction processes to achieving promotion as a learning and teaching practitioner. Staff development is predicated on the culture of the university; this will include the active liaison between the student union and the teaching faculty, ensuring that the student voice is heard and met with an effective response. Some institutions have student-led awards for learning and teaching and maybe also internal staff institutional awards for teaching. It is important to recognise the importance this plays in determining a culture which places emphasis on teaching and learning and provides recognition for practitioners.

In many HEIs academics new to the institution will be encouraged to either enrol on a preparatory course for teaching practice if new to teaching or to pursue recognition within the Professional Standards Framework UK which is run by Advance HE. This is not only valuable for the practitioner in gaining skills and extending their networks but also is one of the measures institutions use to demonstrate engagement with teaching excellence. This can be problematic in that it can feel as though the outcome of measured engagement with staff development is the focus rather than the practice of learning and teaching.

Most HEIs will have a part of the university, usually at the centre which manages accreditation and preparation for teaching, which also runs workshops, conferences and internal events designed to enable sharing and embedding of good practice. To make these types of educational programmes useful and effective for academics one should ensure that they encompass interaction and reflection and that they have been designed with the consultation of the participants to best meet their needs. What must be borne in mind is that the likelihood of staff attending and engaging with these programmes will increase only if staff believe enthusiastically in the main objectives of the proposed programmes; otherwise one may find only enthusiastic and motivated staff attending the events.

Implications for HEIs

With the ever-increasing use of digital technology in HE, universities will inevitably need to make significant investments in both their digital software and hardware equipment as well as the technical services that will be required to support the various teaching practices taking place. If blended learning is the way forward and more classes are being taught using the online delivery mode, then it is vital to make sure that everything technically is working smoothly without systems breaking down while teaching and learning is in progress. It is envisaged that with the aid of technology implemented correctly, HEIs can improve the overall educational experiences of students by allowing academics more time on activities that will make real differences to student outcomes.

Finally, it is also important to understand the role of the student in the overall learning process. Communication of knowledge and skills from the teacher to the student is an important part of the learning process, but what is as important is for the student to become a more independent learner as they progress through their study period. With increasing student numbers and changing demographics the cohort of students entering HE has changed from the mainly traditional A level school-leaver route to having students from a variety of different educational backgrounds than ever before. HEIs need to consider carefully that while in their pursuit of greater student numbers they will inevitably be enrolling a significant number of students who may not be initially able to cope with the academic tasks that are required of them. Managing student retention and progression figures will become an important issue as these metrics are part of the process used to produce university ratings on the quality of teaching provision.

REFERENCES

Abraham, S. (2012), *Work-Applied Learning for Change*. Adelaide: AIB.

Adams, R. (2017), 'Almost Half of All Young People in England Go on to Higher Education'. *The Guardian*, London. 28 September 2017. Available at https://www.theg uardian.com/education/2017/sep/28/almost-half-of-all-young-people-in-england-go-on-to-higher-education. Accessed December 2019.

Advance HE (2020) , 'Degree Attainment Gaps'. Available at https://www.advance-he.ac.uk/guidance/equality-diversity-and-inclusion/student-recruitment-retention-and-att ainment/degree-attainment-gaps. Accessed March 2021.

Advance HE (2011a), 'Fellowship'. Available at https://www.advance-he.ac.uk/fellows hip#categories. Accessed 29 April 2020.

Advance HE (2011b), 'UKPSF Dimensions of the Framework'. Available at https://perma.cc/UT89-LWDN. Accessed 10 February 2020.

Baldiris Navarro, S., Zervas, P., Fabregat Gesa, R., and Sampson, D. G. (2016), 'Developing Teachers' Competences for Designing Inclusive Learning Experiences'. *Educational Technology & Society*, 19 (1), 17–27. Available at http://udlguidelines.cast.org/. Accessed October 2020.

BBC (1999), http://news.bbc.co.uk/1/hi/education/292504.stm. Accessed 28 December 2019.

Butcher, V., Smith, J., Kettle, J. and Burton, L (2011), 'Review of Good Practice in Employability and Enterprise Development by Centres of Excellence in Teaching and Learning'. York: Higher Education Academy.

Carlile, O., and Jordan, A. (2005), 'It Works in Practice but Will It Work in Theory? The Theoretical Underpinnings of Pedagogy'. In S. Moore, G. O'Neill and B. McMullin (eds), *Emerging Issues in the Practice of University Learning and Teaching*. Dublin: AISHE, pp. 19–23.

Carrington, N. (2019), 'The "Value" of Higher Education Is too Important and Multifaceted to Reduce to Mere Metrics'. Available at https://www.hepi.ac.uk/2019/11/13/the-value-of-higher-education-is-too-important-and-multifaceted-to-reduce-to-mere-metr ics/. Accessed October 2020.

Dearing Report (1997), National Committee of Inquiry into Higher Education. London: Department of Education.

Department for Education (2020), 'Graduate Labour Market Statistics, Reporting Year, 2019'. Available at https://www.gov.uk/government/statistics/graduate-labour-mar ket-statistics-2019. Accessed April 2021.

Department for Education (2021a), 'Academic Year 2019/20 Apprenticeships and Traineeships'. Available at https://explore-education-statistics.service.gov.uk/find-sta tistics/apprenticeships-and-traineeships/2019-20. Accessed April 2021.

Department for Education (2021b), 'Government Response to Dame Shirley Pearce's Independent Review of the Teaching Excellence and Student Outcomes Framework (TEF)'. Available at https://www.gov.uk/government/publications/government-response-to-the-independent-review-of-tef. Accessed April 2021.

Department for Education (2021c), 'Higher Technical Education Reforms'. Available at https://www.gov.uk/government/publications/higher-technical-education-reforms/higher-technical-education-reforms. Accessed April 2021.

Department for Education (2021d), 'Independent Review of the Teaching Excellence and Student Outcomes Framework (TEF). Report to the Secretary of State for Education (August 2019)'. Available at https://www.gov.uk/government/publications/independent-review-of-tef-report. Accessed April 2021.

Department for Education (2021e), 'Post-18 Education and Funding Review Interim Conclusion (2020)'. Available at https://assets.publishing.service.gov.uk/government/uploads/system/uploads/attachment_data/file/805127/Review_of_post_18_education_and_funding.pdf. Accessed April 2021.

Department for Education (2021f), 'Skills for Jobs: Lifelong Learning for Opportunity and Growth'. Available at https://www.gov.uk/government/publications/skills-for-jobs-lifelong-learning-for-opportunity-and-growth. Accessed April 2021.

Dicheva, D., Dichev, C., Agre, G. and Angelova, G. (2014), 'Gamification in Education: A Systemic Mapping Study'. *Educational Technology & Society*, 18(3), 75–88.

Ellis, R. A., Ginns, P., and Piggott, L. (2009), 'E-learning in Higher Education: Some Key Aspects and Their Relationship to Approaches to Study'. *Journal of Higher Education Research & Development*, [online] 28(3), 303–18. Available at https://www.tandfonline.com/doi/full/10.1080/07294360902839909. Accessed 5 April 2020.

Elton, L. (1998), 'Dimensions of Excellence in University Teaching'. *International Journal for Academic Development*, 3(1), 3–11. http://dx.doi.org/10.1080/1360144980030102.

Fanghanel, J., Pritchard, J., Potter, J., and Wisker, G. (2016), *'Defining and Supporting the Scholarship of Teaching and Learning (SoTL)': A Sector-wide Study*. York: HE Academy.

GovUK (2017), Teaching Excellence Framework https://www.gov.uk/government/news/universities-rated-in-teaching-excellence-framework Dept of Education. London: GovUK.

Gov UK (2019), Teaching excellence and student outcomes framework and student choice. https://assets.publishing.service.gov.uk/government/uploads/system/uploads/attachment_data/file/914169/TEF_Year_2_Evaluation_Report__6_.pdf

Gravells, A., and Simpson, S. (2014), The Certificate in Education and Training. *Sage Publishing Company*, Ch. 3, Delivering Education and Training.

Handelsman, M. M., Briggs, W. L., Sullivan, N., and Towler, A. (2005), 'A Measure of College Student Course Engagement'. *Journal of Educational Research*, 98(3), 184–92.

Hanus, M. D., and Fox, J. (2015), 'Assessing the Effects of Gamification in the Classroom: A Longitudinal Study on Intrinsic Motivation, Social Comparison, Satisfaction, Effort, and Academic Performance'. *Computers and Education*, 80, 152–61.

Harden, R. M., and Crosby, J. (2000), 'AMEE Guide No.20: The Good Teacher Is More Than a Lecturer-the Twelve Roles of the Teacher'. *Medical Teacher*, 22(4), 334–47.

HEFCE (2017a), National Student Survey. http://www.hefce.ac.uk/lt/nss/. Accessed 23 May 2020.

HEFCE (2017b), Research Excellence Framework. http://www.ref.ac.uk/ London: HEFCE. http://eprints.whiterose.ac.uk/127959/1/TEF-Whats-the-Purpose-booklet-Josh-Forstenzer%281%29.pdf. Accessed 1 June 2020.

Higher Education in Facts and Figures. https://www.universitiesuk.ac.uk/sites/default/files/uploads/UUKi%20reports/facts-and-figures-2016.pdf.

Kember, D. (1997), 'A Reconceptualization of the Research into University Academics Conceptions of Teaching'. *Learning and Instruction*, 7(3), 255–75.

Kershaw A. (2019), 'More Than Half of Young People Now Going to University, Figures Show', Independent, Education News, Available at https://www.independent.co.uk/news/education/education-news/university-students-young-people-over-half-first-time-a9122321.html. Accessed 1 February 2020.

Kolb, D. A. (1984), *Experiential Learning: Experience as the source of Learning and Development*. New Jersey: Prentice-Hall.

Kreber, C. (2002), 'Teaching Excellence, Teaching Expertise, and the Scholarship of Teaching'. *Innovative Higher Education*, 27(1), 17–18.

Layer, G. (2017), *Disabled Students Sector Leadership Group (DSSLG) Inclusive Teaching and Learning in Higher Education as a route to Excellence*. London: Department for Education.

Lubicz-Nawrocka, T., and Bunting, K. (2019), 'Student Perceptions of Teaching Excellence: An Analysis of Student-Led Teaching Award Nomination Data'. *Teaching in Higher Education*, 24(1), 63–80. DOI:10.1080/13562517.2018.1461620.

MacDonald, C. J., Stodel, E. J., Thompson, T. L., Muirhead, W., Hinton, C., Carson, B., and Banit, E. (2005), Addressing the E-Learning Contradiction: Encyclopaedia of Distance Learning (Second Edition), 33–39, Available at https://books.google.co.uk/books?id=sC9Le3jIwzIC&pg=PA245&dq=Kearsley,+G.+(2002)+Is+online+learning+for+everybody?+Educational+Technology,&hl=en&sa=X&ved=0ahUKEwiKmormvJXpAhVTTsAKHYZADJMQ6AEIJzAA#v=onepage&q=Kearsley%2C%20G.%20(2002)%20Is%20online%20learning%20for%20everybody%3F%20Educational%20Technology%2C&f=false. Accessed 3 February 2020.

Marr, B. (2019), How Is AI Used in Education-Real World Examples of Today and a Peek into the Future. https://bernardmarr.com/default.asp?contentID=1541. Accessed 9 June 2020.

Minsky, C. (2016), Highest and Lowest Graduate Earners by Degree Subject in the UK. Times Higher Education, 13 April 2016. Available at https://www.timeshighereducation.com/student/news/highest-and-lowest-graduate-earners-degree-subject-uk. Accessed April 2021.

Mohd, I. H., Aluwi, A. H., Hussein, N., and Omar, M. K. (2016), 'Enhancing student's Engagement through Blended Learning Satisfaction and Lecturer Support'. In *Engineers Institute of Electrical and Electronics (IEEE) (Ed.), 2016 IEEE 8th International Conference on Engineering Education (ICEED2016): 'Enhancing Engineering Education Through Academia-Industry Collaboration'*, pp. 175–80. Red Hook, NY: Curran Associates, Inc Kuala Lumpur, Malaysia, 7–8 December 2016.

National Union of Students (2017), Available at https://www.nus.org.uk/en/news/three-things-you-need-to-know-about-the-teaching-excellence-frameworkand-one-thing-you-can-do-to-change-it/. Accessed 12 August 2020.

Neves, J. and Hewitt, R. (2020), Student Academic Experience Survey 2020, *Advance HE and Hepi*. Available at https://www.hepi.ac.uk/wp-content/uploads/2020/06/The-Student-Academic-Experience-Survey-2020.pdf. Accessed March 2021.

Norris, S. P. (2000), 'The Pale of Consideration When Seeking Sources of Teaching Expertise'. *American Journal of Education*, 108, 167–95.

NUS/ QAA (2012), Student Experience Research 2012. https://www.nus.org.uk/PageFi les/12238/2012_NUS_QAA_Independent_Learning_and_Contact_Hours.pdf. Accessed on 1 July 2020.

Office for Students (2018a), https://www.officeforstudents.org.uk/advice-and-guidance/ skills-and-employment/apprenticeships/. Accessed on 5 Septmber 2020.

Office for Students (2018b), Value for Money: The Student Perspective. Available at https://www.officeforstudents.org.uk/media/7ebb7703-9a6b-414c-a798-75816 fc4ef33/value-for-money-the-student-perspective-final-final-final.pdf. Accessed October 2020.

Office for Students (2019), Office for Students' Value for Money Strategy 2019–2021. Available at https://www.officeforstudents.org.uk/media/336c258b-d94c-4f15-af0a- 42e1be8f66a1/ofs-vfm-strategy.pdf. Accessed October 2020.

O'Leary, M., and Wood, P. (2018), 'Reimagining teaching Excellence: Why Collaboration, Rather Than Competition, Holds the Key to Improving Teaching and Learning in Higher Education'. *Education Review*. DOI:10.1080/00131911.2019.1524203 https:// www.researchgate.net/publication/328124089_Reimagining_teaching_excel- lence_why_collaboration_rather_than_competition_holds_the_key_to_improving_ teaching_and_learning_in_higher_education. Accessed 2 June 2020.

O'Neill, G., and McMahon, T. (2005), 'Student-Centred Learning: What Does It Mean for Students and Lecturers?' In *Emerging Issues in the Practice of University Learning and Teaching*. Dublin: AISHE, p.33.

Roueche, J, Milliron, M. D., and Roueche, S. D. (1995), *Practical Magic: On the Front Lines of Teaching Excellence*. Washington, DC: College Community Press.

Schön, D. (1983), *The Reflective Practitioner*. San Francisco, CA: Jossey-Bass.

Tavaras, O. (2014), 'The Concept of Excellence'. In *The Concept of Excellence in Higher Education*, European Association for Quality Assurance in Higher Education, pp. 23–26. Available at https://www.enqa.eu/wp-content/uploads/ENQA-Excelle nce-WG-Report_The-Concept-of-Excellence-in-Higher-Education.pdf. Accessed 1 October 2020.

Turnbull, S. (2018), A Guide to UK League Tables in Higher Education, HEPI Report 101. Available at https://www.hepi.ac.uk/2018/01/04/guide-uk-league-tables-hig her-education/. Accessed April 2021.

Universities UK (2018), Flexible Learning the Current State of Play in Higher Education. London: UUK. Available at https://www.universitiesuk.ac.uk/policy-and-analysis/ reports/Documents/2018/flexible-learning-the-current-state-of-play-in-higher-educat ion.pdf. Accessed 3 July 2020.

Universities UK (2019), Government Is Wrong to Focus on Future Salaries – New Survey of Students and Graduates Suggests. Available at https://www.universitiesuk.ac.uk/ news/Pages/Government-is-wrong-to-focus-on-future-salaries-%E2%80%93-new-sur vey-of-students-and-graduates-suggests.aspx. Accessed April 2021.

University awards ideas bank (2019), 'Course and Curriculum Design: Award Winner and Runners-Up'. *The Guardian*, https://www.theguardian.com/education/2019/ apr/10/course-and-curriculum-design-award-winner-and-runners-up. Accessed 10 January 2020.

Veresov, N. (2016), 'The History of the Reception of Vygotsky's Paper on Play in Russia and the West'. *International Research in Early Childhood Education*, 7(2), 27–29.

Williamson, G. (2021), Pioneering Reforms to Boost Skills and Jobs: Department for Education and The Rt Hon Gavin Williamson. Available at https://www.gov.uk/government/news/pioneering-reforms-to-boost-skills-and-jobs. Accessed April 2021.

Wood, M., and Su, F. (2017), 'What Makes an Excellent Lecturer? Academics' Perspectives on the Discourse of "Teaching Excellence" in Higher Education'. *Journal of Teaching in Higher Education*, 22(4), 7–11.

INDEX

9 781839 981975